MERCY FLOWS

Reflections of a Married Priest

Fr. Rod Damico

Resurrection Press
An Imprint of
CATHOLIC BOOK PUBLISHING CO.
Totowa • New Jersey

First published in March, 2004 by

Catholic Book Publishing/Resurrection Press

77 West End Road

Totowa, NJ 07512

ISBN 1-878718-82-7

Library of Congress Catalog Card Number: 2003104519

Cover photo by Anton deFlon

Cover design by Beth DeNapoli

Printed in the United States of America

1 2 3 4 5 6 7 8 9

*This book is dedicated to
the Sisters of St. Francis of Tiffin, Ohio,
who made the writing of this book possible
and to my mother Madalyn
and my father Michael, who made me possible.*

Acknowledgments

One can do little in this life without the support and encouragement of others. And though perhaps what I have done in the writing of this book is little indeed, it could not have been done without—my loving family, who gave me the time and space necessary to reflect, rest and write; members of the St. Mary parish staff, who encouraged me to use my gifts for writing and then covered for me when I did; the Tiffin Franciscans, whose hospitality provided the nurturing environment necessary to give birth to a dream; the St. Mary's Writers' Club, those dear friends who so often inspire me by their love for the written word; and especially Emilie Cerar, my friend and editor, who believed in this project from the beginning and who along with the dedicated staff at Catholic Book Publishing worked hard to bring it to completion.

Contents

Acknowledgments 4

Introduction 7

Part I: MEMORIES MATTER 11

"Golly!" 12

Love and the Breaking of Wind 18

My Old "Flammy" 21

A Father Becomes a Fool 27

Leaving Grandpa Behind 33

Part II: CIRCUMSTANCES SPEAK 39

A Manly Cup 40

Fr. Rod and His "Sister" Mary 44

"It's Nice to Have a Priest Who Understands" 50

"Aren't You the Married Priest?" 54

Of Wind and Spirit 61

The Best of Both Worlds 66

The Oddball 69

Part III: SURPRISES SHAKE LOOSE 75

Four-Thirty on Friday 76

"Keep Those Babies Coming!" 80

"How Can Your Father Be a Father?" 84

"I Think You Need Glasses!" 88

Coming of Age 93

A Mother's Gift   99
"What the Hell Happened to You?"   102

Part IV: MENTORS NURTURE   109
"Here's a Dollar for You"   110
"Rod, No!"   117
Why I'm a Vegetarian   121
"They're Going to Remove My Bowels?"   125
Solitude and Service   129
A Lasting Legacy   136
A Tribute to Brother Francis   143
In Memory of Her   148

POSTSCRIPT   153
"What Are You Doing Here?"   154

❧ Introduction ❧

A FEW years ago I was on retreat at the Abbey of the Genesee in upstate New York. The daily schedule there included a mid-morning lecture on the spiritual life presented by one of the monks. However, since attendance was optional, the first few days I opted for a walk in the fields instead of the lecture. I felt the walk would do me more good than the talk. However, one day I made the mistake of imagining a poor monk lecturing his heart out to a room full of empty chairs. The next thing I knew I was sitting in one of those chairs waiting for the lecture to begin. The monk announced that his topic for the day was the practice of *lectio divina* (sacred reading). This discipline is a regular part of the monks' daily schedule at Genesee. In fact, several hours are devoted to it each day.

Basically, *lectio divina* involves a slow, prayerful reading of the scriptures, or some other sacred writing, coupled with reflection on the particular words or concepts that capture one's attention as one reads. The insights gained in this reflection lead to the offering of a brief prayer and perhaps even to the silence of contemplation. The practice of *lectio divina* is taken up with the expectation that God will speak to the reader through the inspired texts. That *lectio divina* has been a popular form of prayer among Christians for as long as there have been Christians suggests that this expectation has been fulfilled quite often. Therefore, it is definitely something worth learning about.

However, since I was already well acquainted with the practice, I quickly concluded that I would have been better off passing up this lecture as I had all the others. But as I sat there wondering how I might make a graceful exit, the monk said something that captured my attention. With stark simplicity he declared, "Though *lectio divina* is indeed a wonderful form of prayer, it really does little good to learn to recognize God speaking in the sacred texts if one does not also learn to recognize God speaking in the text of one's life."

These words snapped me out of my escape-planning mode. Suddenly I found myself being addressed quite personally by someone other than the monk. It was that same someone who had spoken to a young woman long ago through an angel, telling her that her life would be the birthing place of something sacred, and that she should call that something sacred Jesus, for he would save his people from their sins. Now, that same someone was speaking to me, telling me that something sacred was being brought to birth in my life too, and that it was time I began paying attention to it. So along with the Scriptures, I began to practice *lectio divina* on the stuff of my life. As I called to mind my various life experiences, certain aspects of those experiences began to capture my attention. And sure enough, as I reflected on these things, I found myself being addressed by the God who had been with me through it all. The results have been immensely fruitful.

This book is intended to pass on to others what has been of benefit to me. The reflections offered here are the results of spiritual reflection on the stuff of my life. By sharing them I am hoping to show that this is something that can be done by anyone who is interested in spiritual growth. I am convinced that such modeling is important. For in my work with various groups within the Church over the years, I have found that while many people know a great deal about the Christian faith, not nearly so many have any clear sense of how this faith relates to their every-day experiences. This is true of clergy and laity alike. Yet the Christian faith has mostly to do with the living of life. So it is essential to learn to integrate one's thinking about God with one's life experience. As the monk said, it does no good to learn to recognize God speaking in the sacred text of scripture if one does not also learn to recognize God speaking in the sacred text of one's life. Hopefully, as readers see how I have done this they will get a better sense of how they might take up this delightful work themselves.

I realize that my life is a little different from the lives of most. I am a married Roman Catholic priest, a former United Methodist minister ordained by special permission of the Holy Father. In this sense I am something of an oddball. But then who doesn't have some unusual quirk or circumstance that makes their life unique? My guess is that those who know me would tell you that my being a Catholic priest who is married with four children is not really the most distinctive feature of my life. There is something singular about all our lives. Yet the fact that we are human means that we have much in common. So we can learn from one another.

What I hope to teach through this collection of reflections is that *memories matter,* especially those memories that stick with us throughout our lives. Such memories stick because they mean something to us. And it is important to give them some attention. It is also important to pay heed to the various life circumstances that help shape who we are and what we do. Those *circumstances speak* and if we listen to them and to the One who accompanies us through them, we will come to a much greater sense of the meaning and purpose of our lives. It is also true that *surprises shake loose.* Things happen that are unexpected, that open us up to new possibilities for life. In such surprises God speaks to us and if we are wise we will try to listen well. Thankfully God sends us various people in life who help us to listen and to learn. These *mentors nurture* us in ways we are often unaware of unless we take the time to reflect upon their significance for our lives. The memories, the circumstances, the surprises, and the mentors all hold treasures for us, various insights into life that will help us to grow as the people of God.

So I risk a little embarrassment in what follows to offer an example of how those treasures can be mined through such spiritual reflection. I must warn you that because it is the real stuff of life I have reflected on, as you read you may burst out laughing or crying from time to time. You may find yourself grunting or groaning on occasion. You may even find yourself letting loose with some expletive expressing surprise, disgust, or even delight. So it may be good for you to take this book to some out of the way place, where you can avoid disturbing others and at least for a little while remain undisturbed yourself. I think it is there that you will benefit most from what I have to share with you.

Part I

MEMORIES MATTER

❧ "Golly!" ❧

I HAVE a certain memory from childhood that is admittedly a bit fuzzy. After all, I was only three years old when the experience that birthed it happened. But it's an incident well remembered in the Damico family legend. And I remember enough of it myself to know that, as with most legends, there is some underlying truth to it.

As the story goes, I had accompanied my mother and my aunt to my parents' bedroom. They were seeking out a bottle of whiskey that had been stashed away there for very special occasions. I can't remember what the occasion was, but then it really doesn't matter, since what happened in that room has been of far more enduring significance than whatever the celebration was that the whiskey was intended to enliven.

The bottle was found, to the great joy of the two sisters, though at the age of three, I really couldn't understand what all the fuss was about. Then it happened. My Aunt Gloria (or, Aunt Glory as we always called her) got that impish grin on her face. It was a look with which I was quite familiar. Of all the people that surrounded us in our extended family during my growing up years, Aunt Glory was the one who laughed the most. (I think she is also the one who cried the most, but that's a different story.) She was known to play little jokes on people from time to time. And that grin on her face signaled that she had just come up with a good one. She whispered something to my mother. At first, my mother hesitated. She was definitely the most serious minded of the Buzzelli clan. But her older sister Gloria always seemed to have some strange power over her. She was able to convince mom to do things that would have been strongly rejected if suggested by another. So, after a few more whispers, my mother was smiling rather impishly too.

Having received the maternal nod of approval, Aunt Glory held up that bottle of whiskey in front of me and said, "Would you like to taste it?" Since she was one who loved things that tasted good and had often shared those good things with me, I immediately responded, "Yes!" Then she gave me a taste of the stuff. When that fiery liquid hit my throat, my eyes opened wide, I slapped my thigh and uttered the memorable word— "GOLLY!" In response, my mom and aunt laughed harder than I had ever seen anyone laugh before. And when I finally caught the joke of it, I started laughing too.

Of course, the rest of the family heard the commotion and wondered what in the world was going on up there. So the story had to be told. Then everyone laughed just about as hard as mom and Aunt Glory had. Because of my remarkable expression of amazement, whatever it was we had gathered to celebrate turned into an even greater celebration than anticipated. The ordinary had been transformed into the extraordinary, all because I had been surprised enough by a taste of whiskey to slap my leg and say, "GOLLY!"

Though this was probably not the first extraordinary experience to contribute something of enduring significance to my life, it is the first I can remember. Since then, like most everyone else, I have experienced many other astonishing events, and after moving beyond the influence of the Little Rascal's Alfalfa, "golly" was replaced with "wow" or "holy cow" or other expressions that the reader has undoubtedly heard but are better left unprinted. The important thing is not the particular word used to express it, but the experience of amazement itself. Such experiences add something to life that is immediately enriching and wonderfully suggestive of future possibilities.

One doesn't have to think too hard to remember these experiences either. As I sit here writing, the "golly" moments come to me as quickly and abundantly as the water that comes out of a faucet when you turn it on full force. Here are some random recollections of the "golly" moments of my life:

When I went to my first ball game at Cleveland Stadium with my dad and saw all my heroes play in person.

When I hit a home run for the first time.

When I first heard the roaring of Niagara Falls.

When I had my first personal encounter with God.

When I saw Mary (who is now my wife) for the first time.

When Mary first said, "I love you too."

When I sat in a professor's office at Yale for the first time.

When I saw the Rocky Mountains for the first time (and every time since).

When our first child was born.

When I read Catherine of Siena's *Dialogue* for the first time.

When I realized I had to leave the Methodist ministry to become a Roman Catholic.

When after months of searching, I was finally offered a job.

When I saw Yellowstone for the first time.

When the letter from the Pope finally came saying I could be ordained.

When I was ordained a priest.

When I completed my first hundred-mile bike ride.

When I felt shivers going through my entire body as Pope John Paul II's helicopter came in for a landing at World Youth Day in Denver.

When I saw Christopher's tee shot go right into the hole some 120 yards away.

When I saw the cliff dwellings at Mesa Verde.

When I explored the Internet for the first time.

When I saw the endless miles of stone fences and the ancient ruins of monasteries and churches in the fields of Ireland.

When I said to my wife, after twenty-five years of marriage, "I'd like to go away for a month to write and pray and get some perspective on my life, but I just don't see how I can leave you and the kids for that long," and she said, "Why not?"

We all have "golly" moments. They are the moments when we discover that there is more to life than we ever could have expected. And surely there is something very holy about such moments. That's why they are recorded in the scriptures.

The angel Gabriel appears to Mary and tells her that she is going to give birth to the savior. And all she can say is "Golly!" Well, actually she said, "How can this be?" But "golly" really isn't all that bad a translation when you think of it. Mary visits Elizabeth, the baby jumps in the old woman's womb, the Spirit reveals to her what has happened to Mary, and her response is pretty much the same. Peter sees Jesus walking on the water. What can he say but "Golly! Is that really you Lord?" He sees Jesus transfigured before his eyes on the holy mountain, accompanied by Moses and Elijah, and again all he can say is "Golly! Can I pitch three tents for you guys?" The centurion sees the crucified Jesus on the cross and in a remarkable moment of recognition he says, "Golly! This really is the Son of God." Mary Magdalene hears the risen Christ speak her name in the garden, takes a good look at him and says, "Golly! It really is you Lord!"

It's important that we do not miss the connection between these "golly" moments in the scriptures and those of our own lives because sometimes the one may seem far removed from the other. But the truth is that all the moments of amazement in life flow from the same source. They reveal to us something of the abundance of God's creation, the inexhaustible diversity and grandness of it all. Realizing this, we are led to be more open to the many possibilities of life. And life becomes an adventure rather than boring repetition. Even more, they create in us an excitement as we think of the glorious things that await us when we finally move into the presence of the One from whom all these amazing things come. The "golly" moments in this life prepare us for the greatest of all "golly" moments, when we pass on from a life filled with all manner of richness into one that is richer still.

Questions for Reflection

What are some "golly" moments I have experienced in life?

Who did I share those moments with?

What lasting effect have they had on my life?

Astonishing God, you fill our lives with wonders. Help us to see in the "golly" moments of life signs of the wondrous possibilities that life with you holds.

❧ Love and the Breaking ❧ of Wind

ONE of my fondest memories has to do with something that happened in a kitchen long ago. It was a secret happening, only shared by my sister, my grandmother, and me. Over forty years later, this little encounter in the kitchen still brings me great joy whenever I think of it. Of all things, it had to do with passing gas, or what is sometimes more euphemistically called, the breaking of wind. Actually, it might more accurately be called the making of wind, but who am I to question such a time-honored colloquialism?

If truth be told, the breaking of wind was something that happened quite frequently in our household. In fact, a young man who married into the family once said that our idea of a good time was "to pass gas and laugh at it." I think there was probably a good bit of truth to what he said. But, then, at least the good times were frequent at our house, which is more than can be said for some.

Of course, we all knew that there were certain parameters that were to be observed, as there are in any games played for fun. Breaking wind was not appropriate social behavior, particularly at meals or in the midst of family gatherings, or especially in the company of those outside the immediate family. Actually, in one way or another it was communicated to us that the breaking of wind was never really appropriate in another's company.

But really, this only made it all the more entertaining. I mean, if it was expected of us, what would have been the fun of that?

So whenever it happened, one of the adults, usually my mother or grandmother, would engage in the obligatory scolding, though the smile or laugh accompanying the words always let us know that they really didn't mean we had to give it up completely —as long as we observed the social conventions mentioned above. And we usually did.

But for a brief moment that one day in the kitchen, when my sister, grandmother, and I were all alone in the house, all social conventions were set aside. And something happened which was unheard of, even in a household as flatulent as ours. I confess I was the one who started it with a forceful breaking of wind. Not to be outdone, my sister responded immediately with equal gusto. Then greatly to our surprise, our grandmother followed, not with the usual good-hearted scolding, but with her own crisp breaking of wind. The game had begun, and we took our respective turns at trying to outdo the others for quite some time, until all our reserves were exhausted. I will never forget this "blessed exchange of gifts" as long as I live.

But actually, what made it such an unforgettable experience was something more than the magnificent breaking of wind that occurred in the kitchen that day. It was the love that inspired it that I will never forget. My grandmother entered into this game with us because she loved us. She delighted in sharing life with us. It was an unusual kind of sharing of life, to be sure. But, then, this is what made it all the more special. One usually thinks of grandmothers as being beyond such earthiness. Yet, my grandmother didn't let this stop her. Her willingness, even eagerness, to join us with such gusto, was a very visible, or rather, a very audible, expression of her constant and unconditional love for us.

As I reflect upon this precious gift my grandmother gave to us, I find that she did more for me than she ever knew or intended. With her outrageously loving action, she prepared me to receive the good news of an even greater love. Of course, I speak of the love of God. When I have difficulty believing in a God whose love for us is so great that he took upon himself our humanity in Jesus, I remember my grandmother. If her love was great enough for her to do the things she did for us, even to the point of breaking wind with us, then why couldn't the one who is the source of all love do as much?

At its heart, this is what the Incarnation is all about, God taking upon Godself our humanness; God sharing with us in the earthiest of things. In this way he has revealed that his love for us is complete and unconditional. For this most wonderful of all insights into life, I thank my grandmother. And I thank God.

Questions for Reflection

What people in my life have taught me most about unconditional love through their own loving actions towards me?

What experiences in my life have helped me to believe in the existence of a God who loves me unconditionally?

All-embracing God, thank you for sending people into my life who have opened me to the love that underlies all things. Help me to reflect this love more fully in the life I share with others.

❧ My Old "Flammy" ❧

ALL in all, mine was a very peaceful childhood. Family-wise, we kept pretty much to ourselves. We weren't rich, but we always had enough of what we needed. While the more physical expressions of affection were not as frequent as one would expect in a mostly Italian household, we all loved one another and got along about as well as any extended family could. We were spared the traumas of illness, unemployment, untimely death, addiction, and disaffection that many families deal with on a regular basis. So when I think of the traumatic experiences of my childhood I realize that, next to some, they may seem silly and inconsequential. Yet I have learned over the years that no one's trauma is silly or inconsequential, no matter how innocuous it may seem to some. All such experiences contribute something to the shaping of a person's life.

Such is the case with one particular trauma of my childhood that, for some reason, was never filed away in the irretrievable section of the brain where most childhood memories eventually go. It continues to resurface from time to time like a recurring bad dream. Only this was no dream. It really happened. The whole extended family was present for this real life disaster, though I am probably the only who remembers it.

I can still see it quite plainly. Everyone is seated around the table, too stuffed to move after a fine holiday dinner. So while I have a captive audience, I decide that this would be a good time to impress them with my piano playing. I pluck out the tune "Mary had a Little Lamb" and everyone smiles, applauds, and compliments me on how well I play for someone my age. With such a receptive crowd, I am eager to impress them with another of my many talents. So, intending to show them how well I can read for one so young, I take my aunt's music book over to the table and open it up to a song. Then I say to my aunt, "Look. It says *My Old 'Flammy.'* "

All of a sudden my aunt starts to laugh with that great laugh of hers. Then everybody joins in the laughter. They laugh so hard the table shakes. With the tears of laughter flowing down her cheeks my aunt says, "Roddy, that doesn't say *My Old 'Flammy.'* It says, *My Old Flame!*" And everybody starts laughing all over again—all except me, that is.

As for me, I am totally embarrassed. "It sure looks like *My Old 'Flammy,'* " I say. Then I run for the living room where I bury my head in the sofa, and cry at least as hard as any in that room had laughed. Though my aunt and my mother try hard to console me, my humiliation is inconsolable, unmitigated even by the offer of another piece of pie. In light of the sweet tooth for which I am famous, refusing such a peace offering lets everyone know that I am indeed in a bad way. I, the first-born child, who wants to be so perfect, so good, so smart, and so lovable, have displayed my stupidity in front of the whole clan.

This was a devastating experience for me. And though it all seems so silly now, I still feel the hurt of it. It hurts to be laughed at when you're trying to impress everybody. But what I wonder now is: where did I ever get the idea that I had to impress everybody? Why was such a thing so important to me? Beyond the "My Old Flammy" episode, why did I feel compelled to take quick looks around to see if anyone noticed whenever I did something outstanding in the classroom, on the playing field, or at home? For most of my life I have been out to impress someone, driven by a relentless inner sense that this is what life is really all about. How did such a powerful notion take root in me and grow until it filled me so?

Of course, the possibilities are many. And I don't even want to consider most of them, or at least not too specifically. However, one thing is very clear and begs to be mentioned: such a view of life is the almost inevitable result of growing up in this society, though the degree in which it effects us may vary greatly from one person to another. In some form, it is what we all have been taught. Competitiveness is one of the defining characteristics of the American culture. Many parents push their children to be the best at everything. Schools reward those who do better than the others with special recognition and awards of various sorts, as do just about every other club and organization. Newspapers, magazines, and television programs highlight those who have managed to accomplish things that others haven't. While it is true that ours is the land of the free and the home of the brave, it is even truer that ours is the land of the achiever, of those driven to be better than the rest.

Of course, this drive can be subdued or diverted by the many voices and experiences that suggest to people that they don't have what it takes to do anything truly impressive with their lives. But because it is so much a part of our cultural ethos, the drive to be the best at something dies very hard.

I remember discovering once that a woman, who had come to me seeking food from our parish pantry, was actually bragging to family members and friends that her own cupboard was constantly being stocked to overflowing by her ingenuity in securing foodstuffs from all the local agencies. Why would a person brag about such a thing? Isn't this the kind of accomplishment that one would want to keep quiet? Maybe not in a land where the measure of a life is to be better than others at something!

This drive to be the best, the drive to impress, which has been instilled in so many of the people of our land, is inevitably a killer. It kills the body, or, even worse, the spirit. The stress it places on one's life is monumental. And stress is the underlying factor in so much physical and spiritual illness in our nation.

What the statistics tell us I know from personal experience. That little boy, who tried to impress his audience with his musical and reading skills, became the man who constantly tried to impress the audience with these same skills and others. Behind every class I taught, every sermon I preached, every song I sang, every visit I made, every program I developed, every dinner I prepared, every intimate encounter with my wife, and most everything else I did, was the sense that I needed to impress them. As a result, I was terribly disappointed when things didn't go as well as I had hoped, though almost always they had gone well enough. Instead of being satisfied with my best effort and hoping that it was good enough to benefit someone, often I found myself feeling like that little boy who had misread the name of a song and in the process had demonstrated to everyone that he was not really all that remarkable after all.

I knew intuitively that there was some connection between this approach to things and the deflated feelings and diminishment of energy I experienced after my less than perfect performances. But it wasn't till a few years ago, when I could barely function at all and was diagnosed as being in a major depression, that I genuinely began to weep for that little boy who experienced such dreadful humiliation upon reading the words "My Old Flammy." For it was only then that I realized that the little boy had been infected with an illness that had begun to drain the life out of him at a very early age. And now the process was almost complete.

I do not say all this now because I am bitter about my life; or because I do not love my country; or because I want people to feel sorry for me; or least of all, because I want to impress anyone with my ability to paint a bleak picture of things. Actually, I say it because I am feeling better about my life now than I ever have; because I am more able now than ever before to love my country and its people; and because I want to impart some wisdom that may be of value to someone, regardless of what they think of me. I say it because I am actually beginning to believe what I have preached so faithfully and so vigorously for as long as I have been preaching—that we are fundamentally good, not because we are so impressive, but because God created us; that we are lovable, not because we have proven ourselves to be, but because we are made to be; that we are destined for the best of things, not because we have earned them, but because we know we can't and so have come to accept them as the gifts they truly are.

As I begin to live into these truths I find myself starting to heal. I find I can care for people much more genuinely, without worrying so much about how they are feeling about me. I find I can say what I believe will be most helpful rather than most endearing. I find I can do the things I really enjoy doing without worrying about how I will be perceived by others. And, yes, when people laugh at me for saying things like "My Old Flammy," which I continue to do quite often, I can laugh too.

Questions for Reflection

In what ways do I let other people's expectations keep me from enjoying more fully the gift of life?

In what ways have I imposed unrealistic expectations on myself that have kept me from enjoying more fully the gift of life?

What false perspectives can I let go of that would enable me to better care for myself and others?

God of wisdom, help me to adopt those attitudes and perspectives that will enable me to get the most out of life and contribute the most to it as one who is uniquely and wonderfully made.

A Father Becomes a Fool

IN the Jewish Midrash a delightful story is found that goes like this: There once was a man who made a will saying that his son should inherit nothing of his until he became a fool. Two sages went to consult Rabbi Joshua ben Karha about this matter, and as they approached his dwelling, they were shocked to see him crawling on his hands and knees with a reed in his mouth, playing with his little son. They waited in hiding till the game ceased, and then drew near and asked the Rabbi's opinion about the will. He laughed and said, "That father must have meant for his son to marry and have children. Behold, once a man begets young ones, he acts like a fool!" No doubt every parent can relate in some way to the rabbi's conclusion. And getting caught in a little horseplay is nothing compared to the kind of fools many of us have made of ourselves for the sake of our children.

I remember a morning many years ago. My son was going on a school trip to Washington, D.C. He had packed the night before, checking everything off the "must take" list as he went. However, knowing our family's less than stellar record in pre-trip packing, in the morning we insisted that he do a final check. Being assured that he was equipped with everything a person would ever need for such a trip and more, my wife took him to school. There he boarded one of the several busses in that great caravan ready to launch out for the Promised Land of "as far away from school as one can get." Believing that everything necessary had been done, my wife went on to work.

I had remained at home to get the other children off to school. When the last one was gone, I thought that finally I would have a chance to get myself ready for work. It was then that I caught sight of a wallet sitting on a bookshelf. My heart sank, as it looked distressingly like my son's wallet. I knew he had saved a considerable sum of money for this trip. At dinner one evening, he had announced to the family with obvious pride that because of his prudent management of funds over the past several months he was going to be able to buy each of us a souvenir while having plenty left over to get some nice things for himself.

I quickly opened the wallet and found what was dreadfully expected. In my hands I was holding every bit of money my son had saved for the trip. I could only imagine the disappointment he would feel upon discovering that he was on a bus heading toward Washington without his money. I knew I had to do something, or at least try. So I threw on an old paint stained warm up suit and an oil-stained jacket I always left hanging in the garage for especially messy jobs. I jumped in the car and tore off down the road frantically, hoping to catch the busses before they left. Arriving at the school in record time, I was terribly disappointed when I saw no busses there.

But as I glanced down the road I caught sight of a bus in the distance that looked like it could have been part of the Washington convoy. In a moment of hopeful desperation, I decided to follow it. As I drew near the bus, I could see that it was full of young people. Now, being sure it was one of the busses I was seeking, it was just a matter of figuring out how to get the wallet out of my car and onto that bus. Fortunately, before too long the bus had to stop for a traffic light. I pulled into an adjacent parking lot, got out of my car and started pounding on the bus door. I must have been a real sight—an unshaven man with matted hair, dressed in clothes that should have gone into the dumpster long ago, pounding on the door of a bus full of young people. I guess the teacher in charge of the trip had enough experience with such adventures to recognize a desperate parent when he saw one. Or perhaps he was a parent himself. At any rate, he told the bus driver to open the door. Meeting me there, he graciously received my son's wallet.

Having been taught by my mother always to look presentable when going out of the house, I retreated as quickly as possible, hoping that none of the students would recognize me. Of course, I should have known better. My son told me later that just about everyone on that bus ended up kidding him about what his father had done. It seems that Rabbi Joshua ben Karha had nothing over on me. All the people on that bus had seen Father Damico in a way they had never seen him before. I too had become a fool for love of a child.

As I remember this story from the book of my life, I find myself understanding a little more about a story from another, much older book. It too is about a father who became a fool for love of his children. According to the story, this father had two sons. The younger of them surprised him one day by asking for his share of his inheritance so he could leave home. It seems he felt there was more to life than life with his father could provide. He wanted to go off in search of what he was missing. His father was not surprised by his son's restlessness. Often he had noticed his son gazing off toward places beyond what the eye could see.

What did surprise him, though, was his son's request for the inheritance. A request for a little money to get him started was to be expected, but a request for his share of the inheritance was not. Among their people such a request was unheard of, and really quite scandalous. Everyone knew that an inheritance was only received upon a father's death, or when he grew too feeble to handle his affairs anymore. His son had gotten so carried away with his dreaming that he had lost complete touch with reality. He was asking his father to dishonor himself and the ways of his people. The father, on the other hand, was well aware of the reality of the situation. He knew that by granting the request, in addition to losing his son, he would lose his reputation.

What was he to do? If he refused his son, he could well have lost him forever. But if he swallowed his pride and made a fool of himself out of love for his son, he knew that a crack in the door would always be left open. At some time the son might remember his father's love and return home to him. So he made the choice to become a fool for love. Doing the unthinkable, he gave his son what he wanted. And to make things fair, he gave his older son his share of the inheritance too. Unfortunately, this son made just as big a fool out of him as his brother had. He took what he knew should not yet have been given without even batting an eye. One can only imagine the kind of conversations that went on in the village after all this. And undoubtedly they were supplemented with angry glances, sad looks, or the shaking of heads, whenever this father-become-fool passed by.

Of course, it was love that had driven this man to become a fool. And it was love that kept him hoping that it would all pay off some day. He knew it finally had, the day his frequent scanning of the horizon was rewarded with a glimpse of what he had been looking for—his youngest son coming home. Since the man had already become a fool for love, he felt he didn't have anything to lose. So instead of letting his son face a mob of angry villagers intent on punishing the one who had disgraced them, this father-become-fool hiked up his robes and ran out to meet his son. This led to a further evaluation of him by the villagers. He was an even bigger fool than they had thought. Yet what were they to do? The young man came walking into their midst with a new robe, new sandals, and rings on his fingers, under the protective wing of his father. Besides, the arrival of this happy pair had been preceded by the announcement that there was going to be a great party in celebration of the son's return. And none of the villagers were fool enough to pass up a party. After all, times were tough, and one didn't often get to feast on fatted calf.

Yet even then, this father wasn't done making a fool of himself for love. While the townspeople, for the sake of a good party, were willing to forgive and forget, his elder son was not. When he heard what was going on he was filled with rage. His embarrassment over his father's willingness to become the village fool had grown over the years, as had his guilt about the way he had contributed to the situation. And he had always been envious of his brother for having the courage to do what he had only dreamed of doing. So he refused to go to the party, though he knew that among his people his presence was expected. Regardless of how he felt about things, as his father's son, he had a social responsibility to fulfill. And everyone knew it.

So once again, the father made a fool of himself, actually leaving the party to which he had invited everyone and going out to plead with his son to come in. He tried to help him see the goodness of his brother's return. He assured the elder son of his constant and undying love for him. He did everything possible to communicate just how much it would mean to him for his elder son to come and join the party. This begging went on in the clear view of everyone. Fortunately, they were all too busy eating and drinking to do anything but shake their heads and say, "Here we go again!"

Now this is an amazing story in and of itself. What is even more amazing is that according to Jesus, this is what God is like. When it comes to becoming a fool for love of one's children, no one tops God. One needs only to look at the cross to know that it is so. As difficult as it can be at times, it gives me joy to think that whenever parents become fools for their children they become reflections of the greatest fool of them all.

A little horseplay, the swallowing of pride, the willingness to look silly before one's peers out of love for another is something that connects us in deep and mysterious ways with the saving work of God. I have touched this mystery often in my own life. When I have remembered how people have been willing to become fools out of love for me I have found myself yearning to be with them once again. I long to be with these wonderful fools whose love I have been able to emulate occasionally, because I know that in the end, this is the only kind of love one can always count on. So I am thankful for all the love fools of the world, and for the God who is the biggest one of all.

Questions for Reflection

Who have made fools of themselves out of love for me?

What does it mean to me that they were willing to do this?

Have I ever made a fool of myself out of love for another?

How does this connect me more deeply to God?

Extreme Lover of all you have brought into being, help me to appreciate the many ways you have given yourself so completely in love for me that I may be moved to give myself more fully in love for others.

Leaving Grandpa Behind

ONE does a lot of stupid things in a lifetime. Some of them turn out all right and some of them don't. But hopefully we learn a little no matter how things go. At times the learning is quick. At other times the learning is slow. And sometimes it's both. That's the way it was with one of the stupidest things I've ever done. There was an immediate lesson, but the most profound learning required the sifting of the story through years of experience.

A decade has now passed since the event of which I speak. Our extended family was traveling in a five-vehicle convoy following a wedding in Colorado, planning to spend a couple of days together camping. And we were hunting for the perfect campsite. It happened that those in the lead vehicle were of the more primitive bent. We followed them into a camping area so rustic and remote that no one else was camping there. Those of us more comfortable with civilization could understand why, since there were no conveniences in this area whatsoever, except for one solitary outhouse.

It didn't take long for the group to decide that there would have to be a bit more compromising on the part of the "back to nature group." As we pulled out our maps and began discussing where this Shangri-La might be, Grandpa Fred decided that this would be a good time to use the facilities. So he headed for the outhouse, leaving the rest of us to determine our destination. After a few minutes of community map reading, we thought we had identified the perfect spot. With the eagerness of those seeking lost treasure, we scrambled into our cars and headed off down the road.

It wasn't until we had gone several miles that one of the children in our vehicle asked, "Where's Grandpa Fred?" We let out a collective, "Oh my God!" and, signaling the others, we made a quick turn around and headed back to the campground we had so hastily departed. There we found Grandpa Fred, all alone, wondering where everyone had gone. Of course we felt terrible about leaving him behind. But the sight of him standing outside the outhouse in that deserted place was so ridiculous we couldn't help laughing. In fact, every time we want a sure laugh at a family gathering one of us will say, "Remember when we went off and left Grandpa Fred in the outhouse?"

Now the immediate lesson to be learned from this experience was pretty clear. You never drive off without making sure that everyone in your party is present and accounted for, especially when you're driving off from the middle of nowhere. But the hidden lesson in this experience is only now becoming clear to me. I have come to the disturbing awareness that there are other, more significant ways to leave people behind. I realize now that leaving Grandpa Fred behind in that outhouse in Colorado was nothing compared to the many ways I have left him behind since.

In his mid-eighties now, Fred spends most of the year in Florida, more than a thousand miles away. And the truth is that I hardly have anything to do with him anymore. The fact that he's my father-in-law and that we have never seen eye to eye on much of anything may have something to do with this. Yet, regardless of how I feel about his view of life, there is a connection between us. The bonds of family tie us together. The fact that I married his daughter means that I have taken him on as part of the package. But in moments of utter honesty, I know that in my eagerness to get on with my life and not be burdened with his, I have left him behind many times. As this truth strikes home I find myself cutting loose with the same "Oh my God!" I uttered after we had left him sitting alone upon that rustic throne in the wilderness many years ago. Only this time it's not nearly as funny.

Leaving people behind who are intended to be part of our lives is really no laughing matter. At times it may be necessary for the good of the one left or for the safety of the one doing the leaving. But this is the exception rather than the rule. Most often leaving someone behind is not a necessary choice. It is a disordered choice, depriving us of the richness of relationships—of the strength and support that can be derived from sharing life with another. Commonly, this choice to leave others behind is either the product of self-absorption or the fear of our own inadequacy.

So it was with Moses. Though he grew up in Pharaoh's house, Moses knew he was a Hebrew. In fact, he so fully embraced his Hebrew identity that when he saw an Egyptian taskmaster beating a Hebrew slave, he was overcome with rage and killed the Egyptian. His desire to be united with his people was manifested again when he sought to put an end to a fight between two Hebrews. But when Moses was rebuffed for it, he feared for his life and fled, leaving them behind. Perhaps it was all he could do at the time, since Pharaoh was out to kill him.

However, many years later when Pharaoh was dead and Moses' misdeed had been long forgotten, he was quite content to keep his distance. He had a nice life in Midian. He remembered the troubles he had trying to connect with his people in Egypt. And he really didn't care that things were not going well with them. What mattered was that things were going well with him.

So when God spoke to Moses out of that burning bush about going back to Egypt and leading his people to freedom, Moses did his best to decline gracefully. But, as the story goes, God finally convinced Moses to do what he did not want to do. He went to Egypt, and with God's help, reconnected with his people. In fact, throughout history, no one has been more highly regarded by his people than Moses. It seems that his return to them was their salvation and his.

This is certainly good news for us. We know how easy it is to leave our people behind these days. We live in a society where self-fulfillment is frequently promoted above relationships and social responsibility. Parents are abandoned by children who are too busy making a life for themselves. And children are abandoned by parents for much the same reason. Self-absorption often leads a person to leave a spouse behind, or even God. Or if it isn't self-absorption, maybe it's self-doubt. We're afraid we can't handle the care of our parents. We fear that we are failures as parents or spouses and not good enough for God. So we run from all our relationships, just as Moses did.

Yet God was able to shake Moses out of his self-absorption and fill him with enough courage and confidence to reconnect with those he had left behind in a way that enriched his life and theirs. And if God can do it with Moses, he can do it with the rest of us as well. Needless to say, God doesn't always use burning bushes to get the process rolling. Sometimes he uses things like memories of an old man standing alone in front of an outhouse waiting for someone to remember him. I think I'll give Grandpa Fred a call!

Questions for Reflection

Is there someone I have left behind?

What was I running from?

How can I reconnect with this person?

Faithful God, though I run from you at times, you have never left me behind. Help me to be as steadfastly devoted to the special people in my life as you have been to me.

Part II

CIRCUMSTANCES SPEAK

❧ A Manly Cup ❧

OUR parish staff meetings are held in the old convent. Since there are no longer any nuns living there it is now called the parish center. The place has been transformed from living quarters to offices and meeting rooms. But the woman's touch is still evident, since most of the people who work there and take care of the place continue to be women. So it is no surprise that the cups set out for our morning coffee or tea are usually rather feminine in appearance, bearing dainty floral patterns or other such things. And I have to admit that this presents something of a problem for me.

At a recent meeting, one of our female staff members noticed me having some difficulty trying to decide what cup to use. I guess she found this rather amusing and couldn't resist commenting about it. This led me to speak something that I had been thinking for a long time but in charity had never voiced. "I'm looking for a manly cup!" From that day on it has been a regular joke at staff meetings—the quest for a manly cup among the dainties. And it seems the joke is just too good to let go, since the cup selection hasn't improved any.

But while we may joke about my search for a manly cup, like most jokes, there is an underlying truth expressed here that gives birth to the laughter. In this case, the underlying truth has to do with something absolutely fundamental to human nature. And the truth is this—the things we use and the things we choose to surround ourselves with are not extraneous. Rather, they are in some way extensions of our selves. As such, they are filled with meaning. The cup we choose to use, if we have a choice and care enough to make one, says something about who we are and what is important to us. Though the others may laugh at me because of my search for a manly cup, I have noticed that I am not the only one who spends a little time surveying the cup rack before a choice is made!

At home we have about twenty cups sitting out at all times, but inevitably I will reach for one of two—the cup with "Dad" boldly printed on it, which my daughter Elizabeth gave me for my birthday, or the cup with the big "40" on it which was given to me by friends as I crossed a milestone in aging. These are the cups I always reach for. And I am disturbed when they are missing, forcing me to settle for another. I am bothered because I have invested something of myself in them. I take them up because they say something about who I am and what is important to me.

The reason I reach for a certain cup is the same reason my daughter Ruth refused to take up residence in her room at our new house until the pink paint covering the walls was replaced by a dark blue. She is no frilly pink girl. She is a dark blue girl, a candle and bead and starlight girl. And if that room was going to be hers then that's the way it had to be. A guy who needs to use a manly cup can understand this.

But I didn't always understand it. I remember with great pain how I expressed disapproval because my wife had spent a few dollars for a nice wicker Kleenex holder for our bathroom when we first moved into a house many years ago. I couldn't understand why she had to spend money to cover a Kleenex box. I knew Mary's feelings were hurt. And I felt terrible for hurting them. But it is only now, many years later, that I understand why that wicker covering was so important to her.

I realize now, that what I was treating as a financial matter was really a matter of personal identity. Mary wanted the bathroom of her home to reflect in some way the charm and character of the one who would welcome others into it. To her this was worth a few extra dollars. It was more important to her than an evening's dessert or a trip to the movies. Of course it was. I should have known. And every time I think of it I feel like saying, "I'm sorry," all over again.

What our life experience tells us does take awhile for most of us to really hear and understand. I remember as a child wearing a coonskin cap and bouncing like crazy on my rocking horse singing "Davey, Davey Crockett, king of the wild frontier." I remember as a seventeen year old crying like a baby because the blue shirt I had ordered to go along with my tux for the prom came in the wrong size and I was going to have to wear a white one instead. I remember how excited I was when my father brought home a nice sporty looking yellow Ford Maverick for me to drive back and forth to college.

I experienced these things but didn't yet know in my mind what I knew in my gut. Now, after experiencing so many such things for so long, I think I am finally beginning to get it. I rode and sang with such gusto while wearing that coonskin cap because parts of my deepest self identified with the Davey Crockett I saw on TV. I cried over having to wear a white shirt because it is my nature to be something a little different than conventional. And I thrilled at that little yellow Ford Maverick because it reflected to others something of the person I was, or at least wanted to be.

I have come to see that this is simply part of what it means to be human. It must be so because we are made in the image of a God who does this very same thing. God expresses himself through the things he makes and the things with which he surrounds himself. It's true, isn't it? Much of what we know about God comes from carefully observing and reflecting upon his creation. And as people made in the image of God, the same holds true for us.

This means that if we really want to get to know people, we should pay some attention to the things they use, the things they make, and the things with which they surround themselves in life. It means we should give people reasonable freedom for such self-expression and honor it. And, yes, it means that if you're going to have a meeting with men, you ought to have some manly cups!

Questions for Reflection

What things do I own or use that express something important about who I am as a person?

Am I able to acknowledge the significance of such things in other people's lives?

Sensitive God, to you nothing is insignificant. All that you have made is filled with meaning. Help us to respect all things as expressions of your creative genius and of our own creativity as people made in your image.

❧ Fr. Rod and His "Sister" Mary ❧

THE light flashes red on the answering machine as I walk through the door. A message is pleading to be heard. It's the Welcome Wagon woman calling for Fr. Damico and his sister Mary. Suddenly fear of looming possibilities turns into the best joke I have heard in years. I can't wait to share it with Mary, my companion for some twenty-five years now. We have clung to each other through the roller coaster ride of life. We have given each other the gift of children four times. We have shared table and bed. We have the rings on our fingers and the wounds in our hearts to prove that we are something more than brother and sister. Mary is my wife.

Of course, I can understand why this woman assumed that Mary was my sister. After all, the Roman Catholic Church does not allow its priests to marry. Everybody knows this. It is one of the few bits of commonly held knowledge of things Catholic that is actually accurate. But while the old saying that there is an exception to every rule may not be quite correct, it is true that there are exceptions to many rules. I am one of those exceptions, ordained by special permission of the pope. Of course, this decision came long after I had decided that the Lord wanted me to be a Roman Catholic rather than a Protestant pastor.

As you might guess, this business of becoming Catholic seemed about as ridiculous to most of those who knew me as did the idea of a married priest to the Welcome Wagon woman. And in a sense, it was quite ridiculous! I had recently been assigned to a nice suburban church as its pastor. I got along well with the people. My family was happy. My position as a clergyman in the United Methodist Church made our future about as secure as anyone's can be in this world. It was then the call came.

Actually the Lord had been preparing me for this call all my life. However, the immediate preparation began about four years previously. I had enrolled in a Doctor of Ministry Program with many of my fellow United Methodist ministers. The first course happened to be on the history of Christian worship. At that time the General Board of Worship of the United Methodist Church was publishing "experimental" worship resources that could be used by Methodist congregations. Actually, many of them were very similar to Roman Catholic rituals.

So while I was learning about the great worship traditions of the Church, I was actually in a position to begin experiencing their power and beauty. In our little Methodist church, we began using ashes on Ash Wednesday. We celebrated the great Vigil of Easter, complete with paschal candle and the singing of the exsultet. We found ways to celebrate the Eucharist more frequently. We even anointed the sick on occasion.

I found myself resonating deeply with this "new" kind of worship, which was really very old. The symbols and rituals opened me up to the richness of our Christian faith in a way that, though unfamiliar, seemed hauntingly natural. This led me to a fuller exploration of the Catholic tradition. I began to read the spiritual classics. I took up praying the liturgy of the hours. The sign of the cross became an integral part of my turning to God each day.

Initially, I thought that perhaps God was calling me to work at liturgical reform within the United Methodist Church. Then I was assigned to that new parish in the suburbs. The congregation accepted me warmly. But after being with them as their pastor for about nine months it became clear to me that they were tolerating my liturgical inclinations rather than embracing them. When I finally got to the point where I had to hold my arm down to keep from making the sign of the cross in front of my Methodist congregation lest they get upset that I was becoming too Catholic, I finally realized what God was asking of me. Actually, in my heart, I was already a Roman Catholic. And it was time to intentionally set out on the journey that would bring me whole and entire to the place where my heart already was.

God had prepared me so well for hearing this call that, when it came, I knew what I had to do. It was also clear to my wife that the Lord was leading me into the Catholic Church, though it threatened to turn her own world upside down. She loved being a pastor's wife, and the many doors to involvement this had opened for her. And she was not nearly as inclined to all that "liturgical stuff" as me. But though she didn't like it, what God was doing in my life was almost as clear to her as it was to me. So, woman of faith that she is, she fully supported me when I finally said yes to what God was asking of me. And, eventually, she embraced the Catholic faith herself.

However, almost everyone else thought I had gone off the deep end. People kept asking, "Why would God want you to give up your livelihood and the good work you are doing to go to some unknown place to do some unknown thing?" My usual reply was, "It's a matter of faith. I believe that this is where God is calling me." "But what about your priestly vocation?" a good friend asked. "God will take care of it," I responded confidently. Of course, I had no clue regarding the specifics of how God would do this. While my friend said he admired me for making such a courageous leap of faith, I could tell he thought I was a fool. This was the common, though graciously unspoken verdict of most.

Thankfully, God has a long history of dealing with fools. In fact, if the Scriptures can be trusted, it seems that fools are at the top of God's list when it comes to special assignments. Abraham and Sarah were among the first in a long list of fools that God has called to unusual undertakings. Old Abe was seventy-five years old when he got the call. Poor Sarah! The tears must have flowed down her cheeks the same way they flowed down my wife's when he broke the news to her. They were heading west to parts unknown, where they would give birth to a great nation. The fact that she had never been able to have children and was now sixty-five didn't seem to trouble Abe any.

While Abe actually managed to convince Sarah that this is what God wanted, it didn't make things much easier. For after years of wandering aimlessly about, she was still childless, homeless, and had endured one humiliating situation after another. Why she had even been mistaken for Abe's sister a couple times and had some rather important men making advances at her! Talk about a red face! Perhaps the only time her face grew an even brighter shade of crimson was when she overheard the Lord tell her husband that she was going to have a baby at the age of ninety. Of all the ridiculous things the Lord had said to her husband, this one topped them all. She couldn't help but laugh. Well, at least she wouldn't have to use her walker any more. The stroller would work just fine!

As I think of Abraham and Sarah, I find it strangely reassuring. To be the only married priest in the entire diocese is a very challenging way to go. Being a living exception to the rule of celibacy certainly does have its awkward moments. There are plenty of humiliating situations to be endured. Sometimes I find myself attending conferences with fellow priests and the topic of celibacy arises. Speakers have been called in to provide support for our priests, who have been called to live the celibate life. Of course, such encouragement is good and necessary. But I have to admit to being a bit uncomfortable whenever the topic arises. Though the other priests may not be thinking of me at all, I cannot bring myself to look around at such times. Instead, I imagine all eyes being fixed on me while they all mouth in quiet unison, "But what about him?" My presence at such times, especially when accompanied by my "sister" Mary, seems about as ridiculous as any situation in which Abraham and Sarah ever found themselves.

I do not pretend to understand the why of any of what has happened on this journey of faith. Unlike Abraham, I don't even have a promise of where this faith walk is leading in this life. Perhaps this makes me an even greater fool than him. The only promise I have is that, if I hang in there with God through the long haul, everything is going to work out for the best. Fortunately my "sister" Mary shares my view.

And if ever my faith begins to falter, I find encouragement in remembering those countless "fools" in the history of salvation who did what seemed to be ridiculous things for the sake of some promised good yet unseen. Why even God himself set aside his heavenly glory to become a human being. Now what could be more ridiculous than that? I guess my "sister" Mary and I are in good company!

Questions for Reflection

Have I ever felt the Lord calling me to embark on a new venture in life?

How did I respond? What was the result?

Challenging God, You call us to launch out into uncharted waters, trusting in your good will for us, and that our faith in you will bring blessings to the lives of others. Give us courage to make this leap of faith.

"It's Nice to Have a Priest Who Understands"

PERHAPS the comment I hear most frequently as a married priest is "It's nice to have a priest who understands us." Thank God they don't say, "It's nice to have a priest who can tell us what to do to solve our family problems." Of course, people must realize that simply being married with children doesn't supply one with the answers to all of life's questions. Otherwise they wouldn't be coming to me in the first place. But, at times, even the suggestion that I understand something about family life leaves me shaking my head and thinking to myself, "If they only knew."

To say that I understand marriage and family life because I am married and have a family is like saying I understand Christ because I am a Christian. Both leave me feeling a bit uncomfortable. While I do understand some things about Christ, to be sure, there is much about him that continues to be a mystery to me. And the same is certainly true when it comes to marriage and family life.

Here is just a random list of some of the mysteries of marriage and family life that continue to fill me with awe, wonder, puzzlement and sometimes, utter frustration.

—How can four kids bred and raised by the same parents be so different?

—How can such good kids be so bad at times?

—How can such good parents be so wrong at times?

—How can you wake up one morning, take a look at your spouse and think, "Oh God, what have I gotten myself into?" and then on another morning take a look at that very same person and think, "I'm the luckiest person in the world?"

—How can you keep having the same problems for twenty-five years or more without ever figuring out what to do about them?

—How do you keep from blaming yourself for the bad choices your kids make?

—How do you keep from blaming your kids (or your spouse) for the bad choices you make?

—How do you make lessons from your own childhood sound convincing to your children?

—How do you explain forbidding your children to do the very things you begged your parents to let you do when you were their age?

—How do you finally tell a spouse that something they've been doing for years is annoying to you?

—How do you keep from feeling guilty when you pretend to be asleep?

—How do fathers learn to like a guy who is dating their daughter or mothers learn to tolerate a girl who is dating their son?

—How do you get the line "When I was kid . . ." to actually work?

—How do you learn to make the line, "Honey I forgot," sound really convincing?

—How can you make your wife believe you really like her new hairdo?

—How can you convince your kids that one doesn't always have to get something because another does?

—How do you respond to your children when they say, "Didn't you do that when you were my age?"

—How do you get your children to believe that doing their chores and keeping the house looking good is really a desirable thing?

—How do you teach your kids to compare what they have with their poorer friends rather than with their wealthier ones?

—How do you find something that they *all* like to eat?

—How do you convince your spouse that she/he really looks good when he/she wakes up in the morning?

—Are you really suppose to take anything said while giving birth seriously like, "I'll never do this again!"?

—How do you know when to do something you really hate because your spouse really wants you to?

—Why is it that the times you most need some quiet and peace is when your family usually needs the biggest piece of you?

—Why is it that after looking forward to your kids leaving home for years that you can't keep from crying when they finally do?

If knowing the questions and struggles that naturally flow from family life is what people mean when they say, "It's nice to have a priest who understands," then the kind words are certainly warranted. And if it will help anyone to discuss such things with someone who is often as mystified by the intricacies of marriage and family as they are, then I'm glad to be of service!

Questions for Reflection

Are there times that I really feel clueless about life?

Am I able to accept my limitations as part of the human condition that connects me to others in significant ways?

Mysterious God, the complexities of life sometimes overwhelm us. Help us to draw strength from one another as human beings who, though limited in resources and understanding, are united in our sharing of the wondrous gift of life.

❧ "Aren't You the ❧ Married Priest?"

WHENEVER I am at another parish, attending a program or leading one, inevitably someone will come up to me and say, "Aren't you the married priest?" The little word "the" takes on an unusually large bit of significance in this sentence since I am *the* married priest in the diocese. At least at this time, there are no others. So I realize I am a bit of a novelty to some people. When they ask this question, I'm never sure if it's a question flowing from curiosity, consternation, or conviction. Each one is certainly a possibility. Most have never seen a married priest before and they're just interested in the novelty of it. Maybe they want to ask a few questions about how it happened that I could become a priest, or what it's like. Others are totally baffled by my being a priest. My existence flows against any current of understanding they have had about what it takes to be a Catholic priest. Then there are those others, who are actually making a comment in the form of a question. If they ask, "Aren't you the married priest?" with a frown or a look of gravity, it's a clear signal that they are opposed to such a novelty. If they ask it with a smile or a look of excitement, they are making known their conviction that having at least some married priests around is a really good thing.

During my first few years of priesthood I hated this question, though I knew it was unavoidable. After all, I am something of an oddity. But I didn't want my being married to get in the way of my being a priest. In a way I viewed my being married as having nothing to do with my being a priest. In other words, I was a priest because God wanted me to be a priest, not because I was married. And I felt that all the interest in my being married compromised my work as a priest in some way. So I always tried to deal with the question as quickly as possible, moving the focus away from my being married to my reason for being wherever it was I was. Without actually expressing it, my response to the question, "Aren't you the married priest?" was something like, "Yes I am. Now let's move on to something really important."

It has taken quite some time for the meaning of this kind of response to sink in and make a few cracks in a heart that had hardened. The truth is that to be married is something I wanted long before I ever wanted to be a priest. As a young man I longed to find a companion with whom I could share my life, someone who would love me and whom I would love in return. I had never doubted this deep desire to find such a person. At heart, I am an incurable romantic.

Ironically, the fulfilling of this desire coincided with the fulfilling of another, that is, to know and love God. Not long after having a very powerful experience of God's loving presence, I went on a retreat with the youth group from a large Methodist Church in my hometown. My best friend was a member of this group and had invited me to come along. I rode to the retreat center in the back seat of one of the parent's cars. During the ride, I looked into the rear view mirror and saw the most beautiful face. Later I discovered the name that went with this face. It was Mary McCurdy, the driver's daughter. Throughout that hour's drive I kept stealing glances into the mirror. And as I looked at that beautiful face I was as enraptured as if I had been gazing upon the beatific vision itself. This was a girl I had to get to know.

Throughout that weekend I found as many ways as possible to be where Mary was. I threw snowballs at her as our group frolicked in the fields, enjoying winter's gifts. I got in line at every four square game that Mary joined. I managed to find a seat at her table during meals, or a place in her discussion group. I was as smitten as a person could be without dying of it.

As it turned out Mary and I went to the same high school. But the school was very large and we were in different classes, so I had never seen her there. After that retreat, it became my main project in life to find Mary McCurdy among the masses of students who flooded the hallways of Lakewood High. For several days I took every possible route between classes in hopes of seeing her. Finally it happened. I was on my way to Spanish class one morning and spotted her. I quickly ran over to her. But I was so flustered that I didn't know what to say. All I could manage was a nervous hello, and she was gone. I was so shattered by the wasted opportunity that I could think of nothing else. I guess my devastation was obvious since my Spanish teacher asked right in the middle of class if I was all right. It didn't matter. I was too distraught to be embarrassed!

But at least now I knew where I could find her. And the next time I was prepared. I asked if she would like to go to the varsity basketball game with me that week. Then it was bowling, and, afterwards, whatever else I could think of doing together. Fortunately, we liked the same things. And we liked each other. At a relatively young age it was clear to me that I had found the woman my heart desired. And she has been my companion ever since. It was only later that I realized it was on St. Nicholas' Day we met. It is a feast I continue to hold with highest regard since it was on this day when we celebrate one of the greatest of all gift givers that I received my greatest gift.

However, I did not always pay attention to this truth I knew in my heart. A couple weeks after graduating from college, Mary and I celebrated our wedding day. Then we went off to seminary and then on to my first church assignment as a Methodist minister. I was eager to serve the congregation well. After about a year, while continuing to serve this little church community, I enrolled in a graduate program and became excited about all the new things I was learning. The riches of the liturgy and the spiritual life thrilled me. I devoted long hours to my work, to my study, and to my practice of newfound spiritual disciplines. I still loved Mary deeply. But I was driven to do a good job and to be the kind of person everybody looked up to. And often I began to feel as though my commitment to Mary was keeping me from being the best I could be. More and more she became for me a burden of love rather than love's blessing.

The same could be said of our children. Elizabeth and Christopher were born during our five years in Grafton, Ohio, where I served my first church. Elizabeth was the first-born. She was so beautiful, so precious, and the delight of everyone in our little congregation. Christopher was born fifteen months later. He was three weeks late, which was a definite foreshadowing of things to come. He wasn't in a hurry to get where he was going then, nor has he been ever since! But he too was a beautiful child, receiving just as much attention as his sister, and was just as much loved by us. Ruth was born four years later in Fairview Park, just at the time I decided to leave the Methodist Church to become a Roman Catholic. We named her Ruth because she was born at our time of journeying, going wherever it was we would be going. From the time of her birth she had red hair, and the lively spirit often associated with it. She gave us great joy at a time when the uncertainty of what the future held for us could have been overwhelming. Our fourth child, Daniel was born three years later, when things were a bit more settled. He was the first of our children to be baptized in the Catholic Church. From the start, he was a charmer, bringing laughter and love into the life we shared together.

But as with Mary, these four children, each of whom I loved deeply and recognized as true gifts of God, demanded much of me. Though I actually gave them very little of myself compared to many husbands and fathers, still there was that same feeling that they were a burden of love rather than love's blessing. As a professor at a Catholic seminary in Columbus, Ohio and as a director of a diocesan office, I felt that in some way they hindered my work and impeded my spiritual progress. I continued to entertain this feeling when I was ordained to the Roman Catholic priesthood. And this is the real reason I was uncomfortable with the question, "Aren't you the married priest?" The question touched that tender spot I had left untended, suggesting that having a wife and children left me lacking in some way.

I realize now that it is as foolish to let a feeling you know is wrong go untended as it is any other serious illness. But as often happens, things had to get pretty bad before I was willing to admit I needed to do something about it. Eventually, a spirit of lifelessness had so completely overtaken me that I was forced to admit that something was seriously wrong with the way I was approaching life. I was in definite need of an attitude adjustment. As I began to listen and reflect upon what I had been saying about life in homilies and talks over the years, I realized that the truths I had proclaimed so vigorously had become tainted in my own life by self-centered thoughts and feelings. Hearing these truths with renewed clarity began to break open many of those spots within me that had become seriously hardened.

In addition to listening to the truths I have spoken to others about the wonderful gift of marriage and family, I have listened again to the truths planted in my heart that I knew long before I had any words to go along with them. I have listened again to the truth known so simply and fully by a youthful heart that was thrilled by the goodness and beauty of having a loving partner with whom to share my life. I have listened again to the truth that welled up in me each time a child was born to us, bringing tears of joy and love. My wife and children are not burdens of love. They are gifts of love, love's blessings. And I can honestly say that they have been my salvation.

Of course, the married life isn't easy. Conflicts, misunderstandings, hurts, and disappointments will always be part of such a life. How can they not be when so much of this life is spent together and we are not yet perfect? But I can truthfully say that the difficulties we have endured as a family have always challenged me to grow. They have taught me things about my life that must change in some way if I am to become the person I am made to be. Isn't this why marriage is called a sacrament? It is a means of grace. If we live it with an openness to the grace of the sacrament and participate in it with wholeness of heart, it will lead to our salvation.

I have come to realize, far later than I should have, that the full embracing of family life above most of those other things which we have been duped into believing are just as important, adds immensely to the quality of our lives. I have come to see my wife and children as the pure, unmitigated blessings that they truly are. And I thank God for them. I see clearly now that I am not a father at home and a priest everywhere else. For whatever I do as a priest, my family is always a part of me, and really the best part. It is because they have been given to me that I have something unique and special to give.

So what do I say now when someone asks, "Aren't you the married priest?" I say, "I sure am. Would you like to hear about my family?"

Questions for Reflection

In what ways have I failed to fully embrace the gift of my family?

How are the members of my family a blessing to me?

Loving Father, the gift of family life is so precious. Help me to enrich the lives of those entrusted to me even as I am enriched by them.

❧ Of Wind and Spirit ❧

RECENTLY I joined a small group of biking enthusiasts from our parish for a cycling experience that has become an annual event. They call it M.A.T.L.E., which stands for the Marion Area Tour to Lake Erie. On one day the group rides the ninety plus miles up to the lake. Then, after an enjoyable evening of celebrating the day's accomplishment, they turn around and pedal back the following day. Of course, depending on weather conditions and the fitness of the participants, some years have been better than others. But this year's tour will be hard to top. The first day's ride was blessed with a nice tail wind. Then, during the night, the wind shifted so that the ride home was also supported by a tail wind. This is something that cyclists dream of but seldom experience. I've heard bikers say that in heaven there are only tail winds, which made this year's ride something like heaven on earth.

Anyone who has spent much time on a bike knows what difference a good tail wind makes. The people who participated in this year's version of M.A.T.L.E. certainly do. Those who were afraid they wouldn't be able to complete the ride to Lake Erie actually had no trouble at all. In fact some, who were planning on pedaling only one way, felt so good after completing the ride up that they decided to go for the whole enchilada. It was the largest group we've ever had making the return trip by bike rather than by car. This is proof of what a good tail wind can do.

If truth be told, I was a little bit nervous about this year's ride. A couple years ago I pedaled both ways. The first day's ride wasn't bad since we did have a little bit of a tail wind. But that year the wind didn't change direction during the night. So we had to pedal back home on a scorcher of a summer's day into a stiff head wind. This is a biker's nightmare. What began as something that was supposed to be fun quickly turned into an ordeal, especially for me. Since the others were in better shape than me, and were not suffering nearly as much, they tried to encourage me from time to time. But each encouraging word was met with a searing glance that was even hotter than the furnace blast of wind that was constantly in our faces. Eventually my companions came to realize that I prefer to suffer in silence. So as we continued to ride together they became like Job's friends who "spoke not a word to him, for they saw his suffering was great."

However, as you might suspect, though they graciously refrained from doing anything to annoy me further that day, my cycling friends have been merciless in kidding me about it ever since. I have become for them a comedic case study of what riding against the wind can do to a person. According to them, it wasn't pretty. Thankfully, there are no pictures to support their story. I can always say, "I wasn't *that* bad," though I know I really was.

But this year's ride home was decidedly different. Riding with the wind was both literally and figuratively a breeze. This time there was no pathetic priest pedaling in silence. Instead, throughout the ride all of us were talking, laughing, and launching jokes and jibes in all directions. It was the easiest long distance ride most of us have ever done. We arrived home almost as fresh as when we started. That's what a good tail wind will do for you.

Yet the fascinating thing about a good tail wind is that you never feel it. When the wind is in your face or blowing across you, you feel its force. But when you are riding with the wind, you don't feel it at all. The only way you know the wind is with you is that you are going much faster than usual and with much less effort. When you are riding with the wind you know its presence by effect rather than by feel.

Reflecting on my experience of cycling and wind has helped me to understand something of my experience with another kind of wind. I'm speaking of that wind which is the Mother of all winds, the Divine Wind known as the Holy Spirit. I think it's no accident that in the Hebrew language that gave first expression to the Judeo-Christian understanding of God, the word for both wind and spirit is the same. For actually, wind and the Spirit work in much the same way. Biking has taught me this.

One thing that often bothers people who are interested in spiritual growth is that they don't actually *feel* the Spirit. They begin with the assumption that the more spiritual a person becomes the more fully the Spirit's presence will be felt. As a result, their quest for spiritual growth often becomes a quest for some kind of spiritual experience. They mistakenly conclude that if they feel the Spirit moving within them then it will confirm that they are moving in the right direction. However, the truth is that most often when one is moving with the Spirit, the Spirit's presence is no more felt that one feels the wind at one's back when cycling. The truest discernment as to whether or not one is moving with the Spirit is not feeling but effect.

This is not an easy lesson to learn for those of us who have grown to hunger for sensation rather than substance. I know the sensational stuff is what attracted me when I first became interested in spiritual growth. I had read about saints and mystics who had experienced the presence of God in the most remarkable ways. And as I began to imitate them in giving myself over more fully to prayer and meditation, I expected to experience similar feelings of agony or ecstasy prompted by the Spirit's movement within me.

Fortunately, I had taken up with a spiritual director who was wise to such things. I'm sure she knew what I was hankering for when we started meeting. She had undoubtedly dealt with such misguided zeal many times before. Meeting after meeting I would say something like "I've been praying for a long time now, but I still don't feel anything." Usually she just listened. I think she didn't want to risk diminishing my enthusiasm by speaking something before I was ready to hear it.

But the day finally came when she decided to set me straight. This time when I said, "But I still don't feel anything," she said, "Tell me a little about what is happening in your everyday life." So I proceeded to tell her how I was more peaceful, more insightful, more responsive to the needs of others, and more patient with interruptions in my daily schedule. Suddenly I began to see where she was leading me. No, I didn't feel the Spirit, but the Spirit was obviously doing something with me. As I moved with the Spirit good things were happening in my life. And they had come about so effortlessly that I hadn't even realized how far I had advanced in godly ways until she asked that simple question. I was amazed.

I began to see that the most important thing on the road to spiritual growth is not feeling the Spirit, but trusting it. Admittedly, with God all things are possible, so at times he may give us a supernatural gift of feeling, if it is what we truly need to grow spiritually. But the truest test of whether or not we are moving with the Spirit will always remain effect, not feeling. Of course, if we are frequently giving into temptation and falling into sin; if life becomes too much of a chore, a burden so miserable to bear that we are making others miserable along with us, then we have reason to be concerned. Chances are we are not moving with the Spirit. On the other hand, if we are finding that the doing of good comes easily and that we are readily inclined to the kind of prayer and practice which typifies a godly life, then let's thank God for the blessing and keep on moving joyfully down the road of life, for surely the Wind is with us.

Questions for Reflection

Have I ever doubted the Spirit's presence with me?

What are some of the signs in my everyday life that the Spirit really is working in my life?

God of wind and fire, stir up my life in the ways of goodness and love.

The Best of Both Worlds

NOT long after I was ordained a priest I presided at a liturgy in a nearby parish. It was the first time the people there had been exposed to a married priest. Perhaps exposed is the wrong word. It makes a married priest seem like a disease or something! Let's just say that they had never seen a married priest before. Actually, things went very well. The people were most gracious. Then it happened—the dreaded "best of both worlds" comment. It came from an elderly woman, who made it with a smile on her face. "Well Father, I guess you have the best of both worlds, don't you?"

For one who was feeling rather uncomfortable about being the only married priest in the diocese, this was the quip that got to me the most. My own insecurities led me to conclude that this person was making a commentary on my being a priest—that she thought I was making less of a sacrifice than the other priests, or that having something more than the others made me less of a priest somehow. This woman had touched my most sensitive spot. It was all I could do to keep from grabbing hold of her and shouting, "Do you have any idea what you are saying? Do you have any idea what it's like to have a family *and* be a priest?" As it was, I managed simply to smile and nod my head.

However, time has a way of giving perspective. I no longer feel as though I am being persecuted when someone makes the "best of both worlds" comment. Now it elicits a very different response in me. Oh, I am still quite aware of how hard it is to be faithful to both family and priesthood. It definitely can be grueling at times. For instance, one day this week I had the 6:30 a.m. Mass; then had to prepare my Sunday homily, work out the monthly Mass schedule, go to the bank to deposit money into the stipend account, write checks, and meet with a couple for a long and difficult counseling session. All this was done before noon.

After my fifteen-minute lunch, I hopped in the car and drove two hours to pick up my daughter from college for the summer. I got her home and unloaded in time to go stand in the rain for the second half of my other daughter's soccer game. Home finally, I had a half-hour to prepare dinner for the family and eat a little something so I could be at the Parish Assembly meeting by seven. Returning home about nine, I had a rather serious discussion with family members about why I was choosing not to watch certain television shows anymore. Actually I was preparing them for what I was going to be saying in my homily that Sunday. Subsequently, I tried to read a bit and ended up falling asleep at ten thirty, after managing about a page and a half.

Now this may not be the typical day. But such days are not that unusual for me, nor are they that unusual for anyone who takes both work and family seriously. Do we married people really have it any easier than the celibate clergy? I don't think so. Both have their trials. And both have their rewards—which brings me to the second point I want to make.

When you look at it in terms of the rewards rather than the trials, then I guess it's true. I do have the best of both worlds. The companionship of wife and children is a great blessing. They enrich my life in so many ways. Add to this the privilege of exercising my priestly ministry, of standing in the place of Christ in the assembly and ministering to people in the deepest and most significant moments of their lives, and there is no denying it. I am doubly blessed. I do have the best of both worlds.

While it is certainly possible that I am less of a person or less of a priest than others, it is certainly not because I have been thus blessed. That I have the best of both worlds is not a cause for shame or embarrassment, as I once made it out to be. It is rather a cause for joy and celebration. To think otherwise is an affront to God. It is to deny God's wisdom and absolute goodness.

In fact, if we believe in the love and providence of God, then we must conclude that the life God has given us is the best of all possible lives for us, regardless of how it seems at any particular moment. And if God gives us any special favors along the way that bring joy and meaning to life, why should this upset us? Instead, it should send us into ecstasy. Do I have the best of both worlds? You bet. And I thank God for it.

Questions for Reflection

What are the greatest difficulties that I struggle with on a regular basis because of my particular situation in life?

How are my particular life circumstances a context for joy and blessing?

O Fount of every blessing, help us to recognize the every-day stuff of our lives as the setting of your saving work in us and for others.

❧ The Oddball ❧

A T a recent clergy conference we had a presentation on the sociological aspects of the priest shortage. A noted sociologist was reviewing some of the pertinent data he had collected from surveys. In the midst of his presentation he asked a question that rattled my spine. "How do you think the American clergy feel about the married former Episcopalians who have been ordained as Catholic priests?" The presenter had no idea that he had a married priest sitting right in front of him. As the only married priest in the diocese, I could feel myself squirming a bit as I waited for the magic number that would reveal how the priests of our nation felt about the likes of me. Obviously, my brother priests were aware of my discomfort. Many were smiling and making comments to those next to them while looking my way. My oddball status as a married priest had been driven home once again.

Of course, this has happened many times in the years since my ordination. On numerous occasions, well-meaning parishioners have presented me to friends and relatives as something akin to a sideshow freak. But on the Richter scale of discomfort, nothing matches those instances when I am the only non-celibate in the room. In this context, the question as to how the clergy feel about those few among them who are married created an internal tremor that registered somewhere in the vicinity of five point one, that is, not enough to kill me, but certainly enough to shake me up a bit.

I found myself doing some intellectual scrambling to see how I could withstand the unexpected upheaval with the least amount of damage. I decided that if the percentage of those approving the ordaining of the married former Episcopalians was very low, I would make a joke of it. I would say, "Thank God I was a former Methodist!" As it turned out, the approval rating was really quite high—sixty-eight percent. Actually, this should have been no surprise to me, since at least sixty-eight percent of the clergy sitting around me had shown their support of me in some way. Yet, even among those who have been most gracious to me, I am something of a misfit. Though I am respected, accepted, and even liked I am still an oddball because of my unique situation in life. We all know it. And no amount of forced graciousness, or even genuine graciousness, on the part of my clerical colleagues can change this.

Of course, being something of an oddball is a well-chronicled experience among the people of God. So in those moments when I find myself feeling badly about my having joined the ranks of the anomalous, I can find plenty of company for my misery. Even scriptural giants the likes of Moses, Jeremiah, and Peter were not too keen on joining the ranks of the unusual. Each one of them tried their best to avoid it. Moses claimed he couldn't speak well enough. Jeremiah tried the excuse that he was too young. Peter thought he had come up with a foolproof scheme when he told the Lord that he was too sinful. But, then, by some strange quirk in the blueprint of salvation, it seems that these were just the kind of oddballs the Lord was looking for—a deliverer who couldn't deliver a message without stuttering and stammering; a prophet who had to preach to people who not long before were bouncing him on their laps and laughing at all the silly things he said and did; and a leader of those saved from sin who was perhaps the biggest sinner of them all. Who could blame any of them for being a bit uncomfortable with what God was asking of them?

On the one hand, resistance to becoming an oddball for God is understandable. But on the other hand, it is itself very odd. Something is not quite right about it. The God of the universe beckons a human being to do something for him, to assist him in the accomplishing of his purposes and the response is a concern about what others will think! Moses complains, "If pharaoh and his people hear me stutter and stammer like I do, they will laugh in my face." Jeremiah wines, "If I go telling people off like some radical dissident, I can kiss a future career in civil service goodbye." And Peter can only imagine with burning cheeks how the boys down at the pub will joke about him traipsing off after some holy man. On the one hand resistance is all so understandable. On the other hand, it is all so ridiculous. The God of the universe summons. And the response of those chosen is to shrink into self-centered surmises about how uncomfortable things might be for them, as if their comfort or discomfort is anywhere near as important as the world's salvation.

The sin of pride raises its head in many ugly ways. And one of the most common ways it confronts us is in the fear of what others will think of us. This is not to say that how people perceive us is unimportant. Wanting to be liked, to be loved and respected, is not a bad thing in itself. And wanting to speak and act in ways that will elicit positive responses from people certainly makes sense most of the time. However, pride creeps in when we allow ourselves to become more important than more important things. When how people think of us becomes more important than carrying out God's saving purposes we have begun to think much too much of ourselves.

In this context it is instructive to turn once again to the one who was chosen to serve as a prototype for the people of God. Abraham became the father of faith because he knew that looking like a fool wasn't nearly as bad as being one. When we begin to rebel about being cast in the roll of oddball, it would be well for us to remember that we are the spiritual descendants of the biggest oddball of them all. The occasional glances and chuckles cast my way when people discuss the oddity of a married priest are nothing compared to those received by Abraham when he announced at age seventy-five that he was leaving home to become the father of a great nation, a nation that would be a blessing to all the nations of the world.

Somehow Abraham was able to see past his personal predilection for social comfort. He focused instead on how utterly amazing it was that God actually wanted to have something to do with him. As he was filled with wonder at the wonderful thing God was planning to do with him, he was able to shove aside thoughts of personal embarrassment. For an old, childless man to become the friend of God and the father of a great nation, a nation that would be a blessing to the entire world—now that was something! If God could pull it off, then who was he to let a few snide comments and jokes made at his expense stand in the way?

The truth is that many worse things can happen to a person than becoming an oddball. And perhaps the worst of all is letting pride get in the way of our full and heartfelt yes to whatever God is asking of us. This is a lesson most of us learn slowly and painfully. At least it has been so for me. Yet there are ways that God breaks through the hard crust of our self-centeredness and opens us to wonder. This happened just the other day when I was introduced to someone as the married priest. He said to me, "I didn't know it was possible for a priest to be married." And I found myself saying with renewed amazement, "I didn't either."

Questions for Reflection

Have you ever felt like an oddball because of your faith?

What has God done with you lately that has amazed you?

Astonishing God, sometimes you ask things of us that set us apart from others, giving us a strange appearance. Help us to see that there is nothing more glorious than being called to serve your good purposes.

Part III

SURPRISES
SHAKE LOOSE

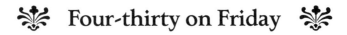

Four-thirty on Friday

IT was almost four-thirty on Friday afternoon. A few parishioners and parish staff members were chitchatting near the front door of the rectory. Almost everyone was getting ready to head home. The bell rang and in walked a thin, sickly looking man with a long scraggly beard. He saw my collar and said he would like to talk to me. I thought to myself, "Oh no, here we go again!" I braced myself to be hit up for some money or a place to stay or gas for a car. Friday afternoon at four-thirty is a very popular time for con artists looking for an easy mark. Like most everybody else, those who deal with people seeking help are anxious to get on with the weekend and are more likely to give people what they want, or at least give them something, just to get rid of them quickly. People who make a living scavenging off others know these things. I have been conned enough times on Friday at four-thirty to be very wary whenever anyone looking poor and a little desperate comes to the door asking to see a priest. And this was my immediate assessment of the man with the scraggly beard.

As he entered my office I couldn't help remembering the con job that a man had pulled on me a few weeks previously. He said he had been stranded in town. Someone had stolen all his possessions. He had no place to stay and no way to get back home. He asked if I could put him up for the night and get him a bus ticket home. The man seemed sincere. His story was believable. And it was four-thirty on Friday. So I called a nearby motel and got him a room. Then I called someone from our St. Vincent de Paul society and arranged for him to meet the man at the bus station the next morning and get him a ticket for home. I even gave the man food for the evening. It wasn't until the next day that I knew I had been conned. First, the man didn't show up at the bus station. Then another man came by saying that he had given this man forty dollars for a bus ticket and that he wanted us to reimburse him. Now, admittedly, I am a bit naïve, but even I could see through this charade.

The problem with being taken like this is that one starts to be suspicious of everyone who comes seeking help, especially when it happens at four-thirty on Friday afternoon.

So when the man with the scraggly beard stepped into my office I was surprised when he said he just wanted to talk. He was troubled about the way his life was going and he wanted me to help him sort things out. I was still a bit cautious, wondering how this was all going to lead to a request for a handout of some kind. However, as the man went on, it became clear that he really did want to talk. He really was looking for a priest who could speak with him about spiritual things and assure him of God's love and forgiveness.

As he was preparing to leave, the man pulled out two one hundred-dollar bills and gave them to me. One, he said, was for the church and the other was for me. I was totally taken by surprise. I had assumed that this man was looking for a handout. But instead, he was the one doing the handing out, and most generously at that. I expected to be taken and here I was the one doing the taking. I went home soon thereafter, shaking my head, with my feelings alternating between amazement and shame. I couldn't help remembering that Jesus had said something about judging not lest we be judged.

As I reflected on this experience later that night I found my mind wandering back to a very different kind of experience. It happened many years before on my daughter's fifth birthday. We were having a little party for her. I thought I would make a little joke, so I said to her, "You know I was five once." And she replied, "Really, when will you be five again?" I have never forgotten that question. It has haunted me all these years. I don't know what my daughter was thinking when she said this. But it was one of those amazing moments in life when a human word and the divine word become one. As she spoke I heard Jesus say, "Unless you become like little children you cannot enter the kingdom of God." Suddenly my becoming five again was not just a possibility raised in the mind of a five-year-old. It was an absolute necessity. When will I become five again? I have come to realize that there are few more important questions.

So why did I think of this as I reflected on my experience with the man with the scraggly beard? What did that have to do with becoming five again? I have a pretty good idea. When I was five, I was not driven so much by plans and expectations. I was not so concerned about things that needed to be done that I short-changed the present moment. When I was five and a strange looking man with a scraggly beard walked through the door it would have seemed like an adventure. I wouldn't have let my experience of a few weeks ago deprive me of the excitement of this fresh encounter. After all, this man looked nothing like the other man. And there was no reason to assume he was like the other man just because he happened to come on Friday at four-thirty.

In fact, there was every reason to hope that this man would be different. Perhaps he was a funny looking angel. Perhaps he was a man with an interesting story to tell. Maybe he really needed me to help him. And wouldn't it be something if I really could! Why, if I was five again, I might even have been able to recognize the genuine goodness of this man because I had not yet developed all the prejudices and paranoia that distort our perceptions. Surely I would have been able to receive his gift with unmitigated joy, accepting without suspicion that it is a wonderful thing to give and to receive gifts, especially when they are a surprise.

Perhaps I will never be five again. I know it is not by straining and making it another project that I will get there. That will only make me older and more tired. It seems to me that the only way to become five again is to stand in the face of the eternal mystery and to recognize that we are really only children after all. Growing toward becoming five again is simply a matter of becoming more and more open to the wondrous possibilities that God sets before us each day. The old saying that God works in mysterious ways has continued to be spoken over the years because it is true. Just when you think things are predictable, just when you think you have everything figured out, just when you think that everything is up to you, someone comes at four-thirty on a Friday and makes you feel five years old!

Questions for Reflection

Have I ever been on the receiving end of some unexpected generosity?

In what ways have I lost the kind of childlike attitude that enables one to delight in the joyful surprises of life? How can I recover it?

God of endless surprises, help me to be open to your wonders each day and to delight in them with childlike joy.

❧ "Keep Those Babies ❧ Coming!"

THE fact that I am a married priest serving in a church which does not normally ordain married men to the priesthood often puts me in situations both interesting and revealing. For instance, at a recent meeting of our catechumens I mentioned that I was grateful to the bishop for letting me remain in my present assignment a bit longer than usual. I further noted that the main reason for the extension of my stay was that my wife and I have school age children and stability is very important for us now. In an unbridled show of support, one of the catechumens blurted out, "Keep those babies coming!" The response to this was a few muffled gasps, a few tentative giggles, a few red faces, and a general feeling that some unspoken taboo had been breached.

The poor young woman, who offered the jovial gesture of support, was a little surprised by the response of the group. She was even more surprised when a couple of life-long Catholics, who were serving as sponsors, pounced on her during the break and let her know that her comment was quite inappropriate. She later apologized to me for having offended people that evening. But she remained a bit mystified by the whole thing. The reaction seemed so vastly disproportionate to the lighthearted and loving intention of her remark. What had she done that had been so terrible?

Of course, to anyone who has been Catholic for very long, the answer is as obvious as it is unspeakable. The concepts priest and sex do not go together! To say, "Keep those babies coming," was the same as saying "Keep on having sex." For traditional Catholics, this was bound to create a system overload! After all, in the context of their experience, the only associations between priests and sex have been matters of public scandal. Now they were being asked to entertain the possibility that a priest having sex and producing offspring could actually be a good thing. It was simply too much to handle.

While one would naturally expect that married plus priest equals sex and children, here we have moved into an area beyond natural expectation. This is confirmed by the fact that many people have assumed and have broadcast to others that in order to be ordained a priest I had to promise to live with my wife "as brother and sister." Thankfully, this was not the case. But for many Catholics it is the case that a priest having sex and babies is something which does not compute!

Certainly the fact that Roman Catholics haven't had a married priesthood for many centuries is the obvious explanation for the strong reaction to the suggestion that Mary and I should keep those babies coming. But I think there is more to it than that. This reaction is really part of a long history of difficulty acknowledging the goodness and desirability of sexual activity, even among the married laity. Born out of a response to an overly spiritualizing gnosticism, which fostered sexual abuses of every sort, this attitude of suspicion toward sexual activity was often adopted by early Church Fathers in their battles against sexual impropriety.

Recognizing the dangers of sexuality gone wild, the Fathers came to view sex with suspicion, even between husband and wife. Couple this with the scars some of them carried from their own sexual escapades before they embraced the faith, and a less than positive approach to carnal pleasure was the predictable result. So we find even a great theologian like Augustine teaching that the only pleasure that is to be had in sexual intercourse between a husband and a wife is the joy of anticipating the children that may result from such a union. Any other pleasure experienced from such a coupling he considered sinful to some degree. Though perhaps pushing a bit farther than others, Augustine does represent a patristic nervousness surrounding sexual activity that has had a profound influence on Christian attitudes toward sex.

The unfortunate consequence is that Christians have experienced massive amounts of unnecessary guilt and discomfort regarding sexual matters. They have been unable to appreciate fully a good gift of God for what it is. Instead, they have been left conflicted. What they know to be true with their hearts, and certainly with their bodies, has been constantly challenged by a spiritual and intellectual tradition which suggests that sex, even within the context of marriage, is something other than good. The result has been less than healthy, an uneasiness leading either to repression or revolution.

Thankfully, after centuries of struggle we Catholics are finally coming to recognize what we should have known to be true all along. A gift of God is always good, wholly and completely. The compromising of goodness comes in how the gift is used, never in the gift itself. The gift of sex that brings pleasure, excitement, fruitfulness, and deepest union to human life must be good beyond question.

Of course, because it is such a wonderful gift, anything that compromises its goodness must be rejected. So sex as casual recreation, manipulation, or youthful experimentation is still rightfully ruled out. But sex between a husband and wife is another story. As a good gift of the good God it bears no taint of sin or evil, as long as it does not take the place of the God who gives it.

So to my catechumen friend, I, your priest, want to say to you, "Keep those babies coming." And enjoy the gift of married love.

Questions for Reflection

What is my attitude toward sex? Do I see it as a good gift of God?

Can I entertain the possibility that God delights in this good gift?

How do I see human sexuality as contributing to life in a positive way?

Creator God, everything you created you pronounced to be good. Your gift of human sexuality is one of those precious gifts. Help me to celebrate and enjoy this gift in ways that are consistent with your good will.

❧ "How Can Your Father ❧ Be a Father?"

WHEN the letter from Rome came informing us that the Holy Father had granted my petition to be ordained to the priesthood I was elated, as were all the members of our family. Our youngest daughter, Ruth, was thrilled by the media attention I received when the announcement of this good news was made public. Suddenly her dad was a celebrity, or at least it seemed so to her. She couldn't wait to tell people that her father was going to become a priest. Unfortunately for her, the news was not widespread. The weekend following the public announcement of my future ordination Ruth was staying overnight with a friend who happened to live just far enough away to be in another diocese. Accompanying a friend to her religious education class on Sunday morning, Ruth proudly shared her big news with the teacher. To her great dismay, the teacher didn't believe her. Instead, she told Ruth that she must be confused because married men are not ordained to the priesthood in the Roman Catholic Church. What a nightmare it was for my little girl—to have such exciting news to share only to be told that it was really no news at all. Needless to say, Ruth was quite upset when she arrived home.

I can certainly identify with what she was going through that day. Even though people see me wearing a Roman collar and presiding at the Eucharist, some still find it hard to believe that I am *really* a priest. "How can you be married and be a priest?" they ask. "Has the Church changed its rule on priestly celibacy?"

Of course, the answer to the latter question is easy, which makes the answer to the first question all the more difficult!

When I find myself in this situation, if I think it will help, I try to provide the questioner with information as to how I came to be a priest. I tell them that I was a United Methodist minister for ten years before becoming a Roman Catholic and that sometimes the Holy Father will make an exception to the rule of celibacy for those who have served as married clergy in other denominations before becoming Catholic. If I still detect puzzlement, I will go on to say that it was a great act of mercy on the Holy Father's part to allow me to be ordained. Knowing it would be difficult for me to disregard my personal history, gifts, inclinations, and sense of call to ordained ministry, he mercifully granted my request to become a Roman Catholic priest.

Of course, even this explanation doesn't work for some. And it's easy to see why. Some questions still remain unanswered like: why doesn't the pope choose to be merciful to others besides former Protestant ministers in making exceptions to the rule of priestly celibacy? This is a reasonable question. But then, mercy is a mysterious thing. It often goes beyond reason and the laws of predictability. If mercy was predictable, if it could be counted on or even expected, it wouldn't be mercy.

In the dispensing of mercy the Holy Father, the Vicar of Christ, imitates our Lord himself who, to a thief being executed for committing a capital crime said, "Today you will be with me in paradise." My guess is that there were many people around who had been more devoted to God and more faithful in their service to others to whom the Lord imparted no such promise.

Jesus had tried to prepare them for such unpredictable acts of mercy by telling parables like the one about the laborers in the vineyard. As the story goes, when those who had been working all day in the blazing heat saw others who had worked only an hour get a full day's wage, they thought they were going to receive a good bit more. Instead, they received only what had been agreed upon, which happened to be the very same amount given to those who had worked but an hour. The Lord of the vineyard had chosen to be merciful to those hired last, most likely because they frequently had trouble finding work and were the poorest of the poor. In his own mind, they were the ones who needed a special gift and so he gave it to them.

"Are you envious because I am generous?" the Lord of the vineyard asked the others. Well, of course, they were. But that was not *his* problem. The Lord simply did what he thought was best and left those who witnessed this bewildering turn of events to figure it out if they could. For reasons clear to him and perhaps not so clear to others, the Lord chose to be merciful in an extraordinary way, and that was that. The same could be said for what the pope has done for me and for others in a similar situation.

Now, after saying all this, if the person still seems perplexed, I will simply lay the cards on the table and say, "I asked the bishop, the bishop asked the pope, and the pope said O.K. And the truth is, I don't understand it any better than you do. All I know is that the pope said yes, and I'm glad he did." At this point attempts at explanation cease and there is nothing left but to stand before the mystery of it.

Truthfully, the question of how a married man can be a Roman Catholic priest is more of a mystery to me now than ever. I have grown to like it that way. Rather than seeking to understand it, I have simply come to accept what is. And I find that in accepting this most merciful mystery, I have become more open to little glimpses of truth, to tiny bits of understanding that are far less than the whole picture, but which are delightful and life-giving nonetheless. In such moments I learn a little something and am amazed at how good, how kind, and how merciful God really is.

Questions for Reflection

What unexpected gifts of mercy have I received during the course of my life?

What should my response be to the merciful gifts received by others?

Merciful God, your goodness to us is far beyond what we deserve. Help me to receive your gifts of mercy with gratitude and to reflect your unqualified kindness in the way I respond to others.

"I Think You Need Glasses!"

IT'S amazing how a brief moment in time can change one's entire life. One such meaning-filled moment occurred for me when I was a sixth grader at Lincoln School in Lakewood, Ohio. Mr. Tassone, my teacher, the man I looked up to and wanted to impress more than any other person in the entire world, was showing a filmstrip. He asked me to read the caption that went along with the picture on the screen. At first I thought he was kidding. Mr. T. was a great kidder. He was always calling us "hot-dogs" or "hamburgers" or some such thing. So when he asked me to read the caption I thought he was trying to be funny. And it would have been funny, except that there really were words on the screen. I just couldn't see them.

Mr. T. was taken by surprise when I told him that I didn't see any words. He was heavily involved with sports. So he had seen me play football, baseball, and basketball with the best of them. In fact, Mr. T. had already spoken to me about working hard at developing my skills, because as a local scout for a big university football team, he thought I had the potential to earn a scholarship. I had been smacking the ball, sinking the basket, and hitting the receiver in stride for as long as he had known me. And, now, here I was in class, not able to see words on a screen that everyone else was seeing quite plainly. All Mr. T. could do was shake his head and blurt out, "Son, I think you need glasses."

To say the least, I was a little shaken by this experience. Not once in my twelve years of existence had it ever occurred to me that something was wrong with my sight. I just assumed that everybody saw like me. But after the note went home and I went on my first fateful trip to the eye doctor, I knew differently. I knew as soon as the doctor pulled down the eye chart and told me to start reading. Even the big "E" was a blur! How could I not have known that my sight was so bad? How could my parents not have known? I guess I had just learned to function so well with my limited sight that neither me nor anyone else had realized there was a problem.

But now the proverbial cat was out of the bag, and my life would never be the same. Suddenly reality had slapped me in the face. I became one of those poor four-eyed kids who have to wear glasses. Oh, in a certain way it was exciting. I, who once was blind, could now see. And it was wonderful finally to be able to see all that I had been missing with such limited sight. But now everyone could see I had a weakness and at the time, this was a major deal!

However, as things that become a regular part of our lives often do, my eyeglasses have taken on several layers of meaning over the years. Oh, quite literally, they still continue to convey my deficiency in the sight department. The fact that my physical eyesight is quite dependent on my glasses keeps cropping up in the most humorous and embarrassing ways.

A couple of years ago when I went for an eye test to have my driver's license renewed, I had to confess to the examiner that I didn't even realize she had turned the testing machine on. Without my seeing a thing, she had seen enough. The eyeglass restriction noted on my previous driver's license was retained. So much for the literal sense of things!

But, when it comes to my glasses, there is definitely more than meets the eye. Over the years, they have also become something of a metaphor, opening me to other dimensions of seeing that go beyond the physical. As I have moved more deeply into my middle years, this metaphor has taken on a richness of meaning that both comforts and challenges me, and in a rather mysterious way has helped me become more fully human.

The truth is that my physical eyesight is not the most significant way in which my sight is impaired. I have come to realize that it is even more difficult for me to see the truth about life, to understand the deep meanings of things, than it is for me to see the big "E" on the eye chart.

Of course, it has taken me much longer to discover my deficiency in this kind of seeing. As a young man of learning, it seemed to me that my ability to see the truth about life was actually quite good. The more I studied, the more I thought I understood about God, creation, and human life. In fact, I was so confident in my ability to see the truth about things that I was actually quite certain that I would be able to see it all clearly one day. A little more study and reflection was all it would take.

However, when I got into my forties, I experienced something even more unsettling than the filmstrip episode of my youth. I entered the wasteland of mid-life crisis and major depression. I began to feel I was no closer to knowing anything about the truth of things than I was in sixth grade. In fact, it seemed to me that I was probably certain of a few more things then than I was now. This was an experience far more devastating than the discovery that my eyes were bad.

Yet as the discovery of the defects in my physical sight led surprisingly to things that enriched my life, so has the discovery of my limited sight into the realm of truth and meaning. As I learned I needed help in physical seeing, so I have learned that I need help in seeing the deeper things of life.

First, it has opened me far more to the truths of life that have been passed down from generation to generation, in my extended family, and in the family of the Church. Truths that have been recognized and passed down, lived for and died for, from generation to generation, are not to be taken lightly. Our ancestors have seen something well enough to recognize its value over the centuries. So the heritage of family and faith we have received must be an essential ingredient in any prescription that will help us gain insight into life. If I remain open to it, I know the tradition will help keep me focused on what is good and true.

At the same time, the discovery that my view of reality is limited has also led me to be more open to those who see things differently, to those who challenge our long-standing traditions, and to those who represent other traditions or ways of viewing life. It seems that my experience as a young man, of excelling at sports even though I must have been using some alternative way of "seeing," is suggestive of something here. All people of good will must be seeing something of the truth, otherwise they wouldn't be people of good will.

Of course, this has always been part of the wisdom of the Church when it has allowed itself to operate according to its own wisdom. Christian tradition teaches us that God does indeed reveal himself through all people of good will, even dissenters and devotees of other religions and philosophies. So, as long as I remain firmly rooted in my own tradition, I can welcome the attempts of others to help clarify my vision, offering them a blessing rather than a curse.

Finally, the recognition of my limited sight into the deepest and most profound truths of life has led me to embrace a sense of wonder. The greatest mysteries of life are indeed beyond the power of even the greatest human seers to see and to articulate. None of us has the necessary equipment. Nor can the greatest truths about God, who is mysterious beyond seeing and knowing, be articulated with absolute precision by those with even the best of spiritual sight. After all, God is God and we are not. So rather than trying to strain to see what is beyond our power to see, it is better simply to let such things amaze us.

It's true, I do need glasses. And even with the best possible prescription there are still things about life I do not see perfectly. But the more open I am to the help others give me for improving my sight, and the more fully I come to accept and celebrate those magnificent things that are beyond my ability to see clearly even with the greatest of helps, the richer my life can become.

Questions for Reflection

What experiences have I had of discovering that I didn't see things as clearly as I thought I did?

How have others helped me to see things in new and better ways?

Am I able to accept my limited sight and simply rejoice in the awesome mystery of God?

Awesome God, the wonders of your wisdom and actions are far beyond my ability to see and understand. Help me so to trust in you that I may rejoice in the great mysteries of life in your loving presence.

❧ Coming of Age ❧

I AM sitting in my room at St. Joseph Renewal Center in Tiffin, Ohio in the midst of a dream. No, I am not sleeping. It is not that kind of a dream. I am here on a "mini-sabbatical," a whole month away from home and parish to study, write, pray and get healthy again. I have dreamed of such a thing for many years, though it was a dream I never expected to be realized. I should know better than to doubt my dreams by now. But I guess I am a slow learner.

By now I should know that God plants dreams to grow and blossom into reality. Yet this one seemed so impossible that I found it difficult to move beyond the questions to the possibilities. I mean, on the home front—

Who was going to cook dinner during the week?

Who was going to shuttle the kids around?

Who was going to help with the laundry?

Who was going to watch baseball with my sons?

Who was going to defend my vegetarian daughter against the meat eaters in the family?

Who was going to support my wife's choice of movies?

Who was going to head up the "Let's go out for some dessert" lobby?

Who was going to tell my wife each day that she is loved?

And in the parish—

How could the pastor possibly do without an associate for a whole month?

Who would do all the Masses?

Who would handle all the funerals?

Who would deal with all the crises?

Who would be there to listen to the pastor vent about the difficult people he must deal with day after day?

Who would visit the hospitals on Fridays?

Who would sit in my office chair and pretend to look busy?

And in the diocese—

Would there possibly be anyone available to take my place?

Would the bishop be willing to send someone even if there was?

Would the bishop support the pursuing of a dream as nebulous as mine?

With regards to the diocesan concerns, it didn't hurt that when I went to see the bishop I looked like death warmed over. It was obvious to him that when I said I was having some serious health problems I wasn't kidding. Being a compassionate man, he was genuinely eager to help me. And being a prudent man, he knew he couldn't afford to lose another priest to ill health. So he kindly supported my idea of a month away and promised to scrounge up a priest somewhere to help my beleaguered pastor. Remarkably, this part of the dream come true was completed in the span of about fifteen minutes.

When it came to the parish part, things went just about as easily. The pastor knew even better than the bishop that I needed some kind of shot in the arm. Also, being a prudent man, he realized that a month's sabbatical would probably net quicker returns than years of therapy. Add to this the fact that I was asking to do this during the month of July, the one month of the year when even those who usually insist on holding their monthly meetings finally give in to common sense and take a break, and it all seemed workable enough. So, after subtly communicating that it would indeed be a great burden that he was willing to bear for my sake (as long as he didn't have to pay for it), the pastor agreed to let me go. Yet another piece of the dream had fallen into place.

But what about my wife? Actually, she's the one I talked to first. For certainly, she had the most important voice in this decision. Also, it was my anticipation of *her* response that had always made the dream seem impossible. Throughout our thirty years together, she has made it rather painfully clear that my being away for any length of time is more of a cross than she expected to bear when we said our "I do's." She has never responded well to my being gone a lot, even when that being gone simply amounted to the more regular kind of stuff, like frequent evening meetings and weekend duties in the parish. She said that she missed me being around, and that she needed my presence and support in the daily running of the household. Actually, if truth be told, I feel the same. I don't like for her to be away either, and for the same reasons.

When you add to this little difficulty the fact that our dreams have never seemed to match up very well, I could hardly even bring myself to share this latest dream with her. Oh, there was one time when our dreams matched up perfectly. It was at the very beginning of our life together. God had planted in me the dream of being a minister and in her of being a minister's wife. And for ten years in the United Methodist Church, this dream was lived quite beautifully. I was a pastor and she was a pastor's wife.

Yet early dreams are seldom final dreams. They merely get us to the place where even greater dreams are possible. And so the Lord planted in me the dream of pulling up stakes and following him on a journey to a place he would show me, which turned out to be the Roman Catholic Church. But Mary never had such a dream. And because she hadn't, it was very hard for her to understand mine. However, like Sarah of old, who went with her husband—a man who had a dream even crazier than mine—Mary went with me.

As I said, after that first big dream we shared together, our dreams have seldom been the same. But we have tried to support one another in our dreaming. For though we sometimes lack the courage to follow them, we both do believe in dreams and in the God who inspires them.

Yet there are times when it seems like it is just too much to ask. After asking so many times for things that have caused anguish, struggle, or self-giving to the point of utter exhaustion, can one ask for yet another thing? Mary grew up as the only girl in a house with four older brothers. She learned to never give in without a fight. So there is almost always a price to pay when one asks something of her. (And the same is true for me, though I have no other excuse than being basically selfish.)

Yet one morning, I was dreaming the dream again. Only this time, after a long period of poor health and great interior struggle which had left me on the verge of collapse, I was feeling the kind of desperation that sometimes leads people to say things they cannot bring themselves to say otherwise. So I finally spoke the dream, albeit in a guarded way. "I wish I could take a month away to sort things out, to spend some time writing and praying, but I just don't see how I could do it." And Mary responded, "Why not?"

Of all the things I expected she might say, this was not one of them. There was no objection, no hesitancy, no raising of a string of questions. What I received instead was a simple, unqualified "yes." I was absolutely stunned. It was as if I was standing in the presence of the Blessed Virgin herself. It was a moment of pure grace.

Those many years ago, when the Lord planted in me the dream of becoming a Roman Catholic, my very wise spiritual director told me she had a sense that all this was even more for my wife than it was for me. She was right of course. The dreaming of a husband always has something to do with his wife, and the dreaming of a wife with her husband. That's part of what it means to say that in marriage two become one.

I see the truth of this more clearly now than ever before. For in response to my dream I have seen my spouse come of age. And while the dream I actually lived at the renewal center was beautiful indeed, the dream I see being realized in my dear wife is more beautiful still.

Questions for Reflection

Have I ever had a dream I felt compelled to pursue?

What has kept me from pursuing my dreams?

What has helped me to pursue them?

Author of all good dreams, give me the courage and support I need to pursue those good dreams you have planted in me.

❧ A Mother's Gift ❧

A FEW weeks ago on a Saturday morning I received an unexpected phone call in the middle of an appointment with a young couple preparing for marriage. The call was from my daughter Elizabeth. She said that mom had just called to tell us that grandma McCurdy was dying. If we wanted to say any final words to her, we would have to call right away.

As soon as the couple was out the door I phoned the nursing home that my mother-in-law had entered the previous day. We had found out less than a week before that she was seriously sick with cancer. When my wife Mary picked up the phone in her mother's room she confirmed that her mom was indeed very close to death. She asked if I would like to speak to her and say goodbye. Of course, I said yes.

But what parting word can one offer to a person who has had such a significant part in one's life? Mary put the phone to her mother's ear. I can't remember all that I said. What I do remember is thanking her for all that she had done for us. Most especially, I thanked her for the gift of her daughter. I told mom that Mary's being the wonderful person she is had much to do with what she had done with and for her. I told her I knew how proud she was of Mary and just how thankful I was that she had shared her daughter with me. And I could tell by the sounds she made in response that she understood, appreciated and accepted my thanks. A few hours later she died.

As I have thought about what I said to her in the days and weeks since, I am comforted by the wordless response she made to my expression of thanks. Annabell McCurdy was a true mother. She loved all her children and had a special love for her only daughter, Mary. She was proud of the person that Mary has become. And she was delighted to think that she had contributed significantly to Mary's development as a person. She had every right to be.

Annabell has deepened my awareness of some important things about motherhood that are easy to overlook. How amazing motherhood is! From it flows the gift of life. Of course, the carrying of the child in the womb and the amazing act of giving birth is a major part of that gift. This alone should make children eternally grateful to their mothers. But there is so much more to a mother's gift than this. Her presence and nurturing adds so much to the shaping of the life she has brought into the world. What we become as human beings is profoundly influenced for good or for ill by those who have accepted the awesome responsibility of motherhood. It is a monumental task, one that could easily overwhelm a woman if she thought too much about what she had taken on at the moment of conception.

If anyone deserves our admiration, gratitude and respect, it is those who have taken seriously the vocation of mothering. It would be a shame to let such persons pass from our lives without taking the time to tell them just how much we appreciate who they are and what they have done for us. And it's too bad that often we wait till our mother is dying to let her know just how much she has meant to us.

Questions for Reflection

How has my mother helped to shape my life?

What am I doing to let the significant mothers in my life know how much I value them?

Mothering God, you bring us into being and nurture us constantly. And you bless us with human mothers who share in your work of birthing and cultivating the precious gift of life. Help us to find fitting ways to support them and to thank them.

"What the Hell Happened to You?"

I HAD a conversation the other day with a man whose mother recently died. He shared a story about her that has been resurfacing in my consciousness ever since. For years this woman had experienced the mental decline that accompanies Alzheimer's Disease. She had gotten to the point where she had lost touch almost completely with present reality, though many past memories were still quite vivid. For the past few years, she didn't even recognize her children when they visited her, though she continued to have vivid memories of them from years long past. But, dutiful son that he was, the man who told me the story continued to visit her.

As the story goes, during the course of one of these visits she asked him four times who he was. Each time he answered, "I'm Jack." When she asked him the fifth time he responded in a rather desperate tone, "I'm your son Jack. Mom, don't you remember me?" At this she leaned toward him, took a good long look and said, "What the hell happened to you?"

Obviously he no longer looked like the son she remembered. No doubt he looked quite a bit older. What was left of his hair was beginning to gray. Wrinkles had begun to appear on his face. He had a paunch around his waist. And on his face, a look of seriousness had replaced an impish grin. Who could blame her for asking, "What the hell happened to you?"

As I think of this comically disturbing incident, I imagine myself being in a similar situation. I imagine visiting my father who, thankfully, still has his wits about him. But I am just imagining you see, so I turn him into a senile old man who finally gives me a good hard look and asks the same question. "What the hell happened to you?" I find myself stumbling and stammering as I try to formulate a response. How can I describe for him what has brought about my own change in appearance over the years? How can I explain why the little boy who often played catch with him on the sidewalk in front of the house can hardly even throw a ball any more? How can I explain my own graying hair and diminished vitality? What will he think of his little boy if I tell him that frequently I fall asleep during the six o'clock news but lie wide awake in the middle of the night?

Suddenly it just begins to pour out. "Well, dad, you know I got married." This in itself would have been enough to explain most things to his satisfaction. Yet I go on. "We've raised four children too." Again this would have been sufficient. But the floodgate has burst and there is no stopping it now. "I left the Methodist ministry to become a Catholic, remember dad?" "Remember all the times we moved? Remember when I was out of work for a while? Remember when I had to wait five years for an answer to my petition to be ordained a priest? Remember when I became the first married priest in the diocese? Remember how hard I've had to work all the time? Remember when mom died? Remember when our first two kids went off to college and our younger ones were in Catholic schools and we were making four tuition payments at once? Remember when I went through my depression?"

I could say more. However, by this time I feel that I've probably said more than he wanted to hear. But then much to my surprise, in his childish wisdom, this senile old father of my imagination smiles and says, "Well, don't feel too bad son. With the exception of that married priest stuff, pretty much the same thing happened to me." Of course, I know he's right. The challenges of work and family and figuring out what life is all about takes its toll on just about everyone, though some seem to weather it a bit better than others.

Then, just when I think the imaginary exercise has come to an end, the old man says, "God's been good to you son." And I wonder if he's already forgotten everything I said. But the light in his eyes tells me differently. He remembers it all. So I ask him, "What are you saying dad? I just told you about all those things that have worn me down over the years. What do you mean God's been good to me?" "I mean son that anything important enough to take on or to live through carries with it a blessing. Why, I'm looking at one right now." I realize with a sense of delight that he's looking at me.

So I think about what this imaginary father of mine has said, though he is beginning to sound more like my real father all the time. I think about that list of things I just threw out at him. And sure enough, he's right. My being married has been difficult at times. In terms of personality and temperament, my wife and I are very different. This has led to misunderstandings and battles throughout our life together. We both bear the deep wounds that are the inevitable result of such a life. Perhaps of all things in life, marriage has taken the greatest toll on me. But it has also been my greatest blessing. The countless battles have worn me down to the point where I have become vulnerable to the truth. Time and again my defenses have been broken through. I have been forced to see my sins and weaknesses in all their ugliness. At the same time, as we have continued to share life together, I have experienced more often than I want to admit that it is possible to be loved by someone you have wronged. It is possible to be reconciled, to move on, to grow and to be fruitful. In truth, my wife has helped me to embrace the hope of salvation and at times has been my salvation.

Of course, being a father is no easy thing either. The demands are constant. My responsibilities have ranged from making enough money to provide for my children, to changing their diapers, to comforting them when they are hurt and disciplining them when they hurt others, to getting them to all their games and activities and then sitting through many of them myself, to teaching them to be independent and then being disregarded or neglected by them when I've succeeded, to experiencing the pain of losing them when they leave home. Perhaps, as much as marriage, such things contribute to the devastation of mind and body. Yet these injuries are small compared to the blessings of parenthood. I know of nothing that kindles the flame of love within one's heart as much as seeing the birth of one's child and then holding that child in one's arms, unless it is holding that child in your arms when he needs reassuring, or patting her on the back when she has mastered something you taught her, or hugging him goodbye when he is leaving. I know of nothing that challenges a person to be good as much as having a child who looks up to you. I know of nothing that enriches a person as much as receiving the love and trust of children through every age and season of life.

Though with varying levels of intensity and effect, what I have said about marriage and parenting also could be said of almost every significant experience of my life. Those that have taken the most out of me have enriched me even more. My being a married priest certainly has not been easy. Yet it has also been fulfilling for me in ways that nothing else could. The death of my mother was hard. But it helped me to receive more fully from the gift of her life. My ongoing struggle with depression has been the worst, most difficult experience of them all. But it has opened for me a new depth of understanding and compassion for people that I wouldn't have otherwise. And so it goes.

As I ponder all this I find my mind wandering to the bank of a river late at night. A man sits there alone imagining his future. Suddenly someone pounces on him and they wrestle till daybreak. It is a titanic struggle. But the man won't give up, even when the stranger strikes him a blow that knocks his hip out of joint. Though limping now, exceedingly tired, and racked with pain the man will not let the stranger go, at least not until the stranger blesses him. Much to his surprise, and relief, the stranger gives him the blessing. Of course, the man is Jacob. And the stranger is God. In one way or another, the stranger always is. Because of this, one never escapes a tussle without being wounded or broken in some way. However, if one hangs on to that stranger for dear life, one usually comes away with some blessing. Undoubtedly the limp troubled Jacob at times. But in the long run, surely it was the blessing that mattered most. At least my own experience tells me this is so.

That imaginary father of mine is truly a wise man. The most difficult and demanding experiences of life often do carry with them the greatest blessings. God has been good to me. And in a strange way the signs of wear and tear that have become increasingly visible over the years are the very signs of that divine goodness. So the next time somebody, imaginary or real, takes a good hard look at me and says, "What the hell happened to you?" I know what my answer will be. "I've been blessed!"

Questions for Reflection

What have been the most difficult experiences of my life?

What blessings have I received from them?

Challenging God, sometimes you lead us on paths that are difficult to travel. Give us the strength we need to persevere and the insight we need to glean the blessings from the wrestlings.

Part IV

MENTORS NURTURE

 "Here's a Dollar for You"

WE all have certain regrets in life. Several of mine have to do with people I wish I had gotten to know better. One of them was my grandma Damico. She and Grandpa Damico lived in the little borough called Dunbar, in the southeastern hills of Pennsylvania. At one time this had been a rather prosperous part of the state. Coal mining and coke ovens had brought jobs and money. But during my grandparents' lifetime the area was pretty well mined out and the coke ovens were closed. Dunbar became a seriously depressed locality, with a large number of people on welfare. And most of the young went off to seek their fortunes elsewhere. My father was one of them.

But my father's parents continued to live there, as did his brothers and sisters and some of his nieces and nephews. So we visited Dunbar from time to time. I loved visiting my grandma and grandpa Damico. They had a small house with a little garden behind it where they grew their own vegetables. And behind the garden was a chicken coop, complete with real live chickens. I never saw anything like that in Cleveland, Ohio where I was born and raised. Grandpa Damico knew that and was always eager to take my sister and me up to that old chicken coop so he could see the look of fascination on our faces as we took it all in.

Grandpa Damico was a kind man. It seemed he spent most of his time just sitting quietly with a smile on his face. I think he was like this, first of all, because it was his nature, and secondly, because he felt it was his obligation to test his homemade wine quite frequently to make sure it was good enough to share with others.

I have to admit, though, that while I enjoyed visiting grandpa, it was grandma that I looked forward to seeing the most. She was a short, sprightly woman, good-natured, with a touch of mischief about her that was absolutely delightful. She always asked questions that would make one of us wiggle and squirm, something about what it was like to live in a place where people had money; or if I had a girlfriend; or who we liked better, our mother or our father. Grandma Damico didn't need money to have fun. And it was fun for me just being there with her.

In addition to her needling my father, who was the only one of her children to leave Dunbar to seek his livelihood elsewhere, and asking my sister and me questions that made us laugh, Grandma Damico always did two other things. First, she would have a big meal for us—spaghetti, complete with pepperoni, meatballs and roast pork that had simmered all day in the sauce. It was a symbiotic relationship if ever there was one. I enjoyed eating and she enjoyed feeding. Almost the first thing she would say to us after we walked through the door was, "You've got to eat. Come, sit at the table." So that's what we did. We ate and ate. But no matter how much we ate, she would keep telling us to eat more until finally, when our bellies felt like they were about to burst, we managed to escape from the table to the living room. The food was always so good and bountiful that the treat of a meal at Grandma Damico's was hard to beat. But this wasn't the thing I liked most about visiting her. The best was yet to come.

Without exception, when we were about to leave, grandma would go to a drawer in the living room and pull out some money—a dollar for me and one for my sister. Though my grandparents had just about nothing in terms of worldly possessions, I always came away with something. I always looked forward to getting that dollar from grandma because I liked having a dollar to spend on treats. But even more, I enjoyed receiving the dollar because it seemed to delight her so to give it to me.

I didn't realize what a precious gift those dollars were until the day I heard my dad tell her that she had to stop giving her money away. It was hard for a child who had grown up as I did, in a situation where we always had enough of whatever we needed, to realize that there were people as poor as my grandparents were. So I had no idea that often the dollars she gave to my sister and me were her very last dollars. Like the widow in the gospel, when she gave us those two little dollar bills, she had given us all she had. That day, when I heard my father tell grandma she had to stop giving us money, I was totally taken by surprise. As we drove away in the car, dad told us that she had always been this way. No matter who it was that came to see her, they would always leave with something. So, of course, everybody loved to visit her. She was a favorite of the neighborhood kids because she was always giving them money or something to eat. The family had talked with her about this on numerous occasions, but it was no use. It seems that grandma got such joy out of giving that she just couldn't stop.

At the time, I didn't know what to make of such a thing. It was so foreign to my experience. I didn't know anyone else who had so little. And I didn't know anyone else who gave so much. When I saw people beaming for joy, it was usually over something they had acquired rather than over something they had given away. I concluded, therefore, that grandma was a very strange, but lovable person. And I still looked forward to receiving the dollar when I visited her, though after hearing what my father said about her, it was always with a little twinge of guilt.

But it is only now, many years after she has gone to a place where those around her appreciate what so many around her here thought was foolishness, that I have begun to receive the greatest of her many gifts to me. I have finally begun to learn what she was teaching me all along about the true spirit of giving.

Like most other people, on many occasions I had heard what St. Paul said about God loving a cheerful giver. But I was never exactly sure what he meant. Giving, to me, was always something calculated. Could I afford to give something? How much could I afford to give? Was the cause or the person worthy of such a gift? Or, when my giving wasn't calculated, it was guilt driven. I felt guilty about having so much when others had so little. So I gave a little something in order to feel better about myself. However, I think most often the driving force behind my gifts was the hope that others would think well of me—both other people and the divine other. Of course, I knew this wasn't exactly what St. Paul had in mind. But it was the best I could do in terms of cheerfulness in the giving department.

I don't think my experience is all that unusual. In our society we tend to be very self-focused. Either we are busy proving ourselves or indulging ourselves. So it should be no surprise that giving most often occurs in this context. While the popular saying "The one who dies with the most toys wins" is not a motto that most people would recognize as their own, it does contain a kernel of truth about prevailing attitudes in America today. We have come to focus our lives on what we can attain and possess. And it is there that we expect to find our joy.

As people made in the image of a God whose very nature is one of selfless giving, the approach to life I have just described is doomed to failure. I know this now, though I had to learn it the hard way. For though my entire adult life has been devoted to the "service" of God's people, I have come to see that this service has been driven most often by the same kind of self-focus which typifies so much of life in our land. While it is true that I do have a sense of compassion for people and a desire to help them, too often the primary concern behind my ministry to others has been how it will reflect upon me. So often I have found myself thinking, "If I say this in a homily, what will they think of me?" Or, "If I visit this person and not that person, what will they think of me?" Or, "If I don't attend this meeting, what will they think of me?" When I reflect upon my years of ministry honestly, I find that much of what I have done has been done to benefit myself, though thankfully I know it has benefited others as well.

Now I realize that some will say that this doesn't really matter as long as people have been served. But it does matter. It matters why we do things, because the why is part of the thing we do. Motivation and action go together. Motivation affects action. And it affects the one doing the action. I know that in my desire to make some people feel good about me, I have actually turned away from others who really needed me more. Calculation often stands in the way of compassion. Typically, I have planned out a day's work with the intention of doing all those things that would make people think of me as a good priest. Because this has been my main concern, frequently I have held so steadfastly to that plan that I have not responded to interruptions or inspirations that were really far more important than anything on my prepared agenda. The needy call, but the day planner has priority.

When we live this way, is it any wonder that we experience such things as mid-life crisis? After neglecting the voice of our heart for years, where else can it lead but to a malfunction in our system? The soul and the body become disconnected (interestingly something that happens totally in death), and the quality and energy of life are radically diminished. The voice of our heart is constantly telling us that joy is in the giving itself and not in what we get as a return; that giving is not an investment, but an act of love; and that knowing we have done something to make life better for someone should be the source of our joy. This is the truth that speaks to us from the depths of our being when we experience moments of genuine awareness. It is the truth of which Paul speaks when he talks about giving cheerfully. And until we begin to live out of this perspective, we will always be candidates for an interior crisis of some kind or another. The scriptures tell us that we are made in the image of a God who gives, not because he wants anything in return, but simply because he delights in giving. So until we begin to do likewise, we will always be at odds with our own nature.

I doubt if my grandma Damico ever thought of her own giving in quite this way. She simply knew that giving brought joy to her life. So she gave whatever she had, delighting in the smiles it brought and the new energy it infused into the lives of others. She was a theologian in the truest sense—one who has a knowledge of God that comes not from books or learned argument, but from getting to know the truth that was always present in her heart. In listening to the deepest expressions of her heart, she was in harmony with herself and with the God in whose image she was made.

As I think of her now, she speaks to me more powerfully than any theologian I have ever read, though there have been some good ones to be sure. She is teaching me about giving without speculation or premeditation. She is teaching me to give because it is what I have been made to do. She is teaching me to give for the sheer goodness of it, for the joy it imparts, and for the joy it is. The more I follow her teaching, which is also the Lord's teaching, the less I am aware of any personal crisis, and the more I find myself leaving people with a smile on their face or a spring in their step, just like my grandma did.

Questions for Reflection

Who are the most giving people I have ever known?

Is the Lord calling me to give more generously or more cheerfully?

Ever-giving God, your generosity to us knows no bounds. Help us to become more like you in our giving to others.

❧ "Rod, No!" ❧

WHEN I was growing up in Lakewood, Ohio, we played summer baseball during the day. Usually teachers or college students, who had summers off from school, worked as umpires. Since most of the games were during working hours we seldom had a large number of fans watching us. But there were always some—a few mothers, grandparents, retired people looking for a little entertainment and neighborhood kids with nothing better to do.

In those days it was a real treat when a parent could manage to make it to one of our games. Occasionally I was one of the fortunate ones. Because my father's work involved regular shift rotations, he was sometimes able to come to the games. It was always an exciting thing for me to see him sitting there in the stands. And it was almost as exciting for my teammates, since my dad was the one who coached us when we got together for practices before the season started or between games.

However, there was a day when having my dad in the stands led to what was for me, a most dreadful incident. I was our team's star pitcher. But I had been pitching too much, and the team we were playing wasn't very good. So my dad had told me that under absolutely no circumstances was I to pitch that day. He didn't want me to hurt my arm. And I promised him I wouldn't pitch.

As it happened, the game went along quite well without me on the mound until the fifth inning. We were up twelve to four. Then, our starting pitcher began to falter. I called time (I was the team's on-the-field manager) and walked in from my center field position. For some reason I decided that I had better pitch the rest of the game. I took the ball and threw a warm-up pitch. Suddenly my dad stood up in the stands and shouted, "Rod, NO!" I was stunned. My dad had yelled at me in front of my teammates, the umpire, the fans, and whoever else happened to be in the vicinity of the field at that time. I knew I was wrong for having come in to pitch. But I never dreamed that he would create such a scene. I was totally humiliated.

The combined experience of recognizing I had broken a promise to my father and being thoroughly humiliated in front of so many people left me feeling nauseous. I didn't know what to do. So, after throwing one more warm-up pitch, I told the umpire that my arm was sore and called in another pitcher. It was an event that has remained indelibly etched in my memory.

However, time and experience inevitably lead to adjustments in our way of seeing things. Now, when I remember that scene at the ball field I see more than I once did. Oh, I still see a very shy and timid child being totally humiliated before a crowd. But the faces have grown fuzzy and the humiliation no longer seems nearly as great for the young man on the field as it once did.

Remarkably, though, as I take in that scene looking through the lenses of memory and reflection, I notice now that there is another person who is suffering a far greater humiliation than I am. It is my father. At the time I was too focused on myself to see it. But now I see it clearly. Here is a man jumping up in the stands, shouting about something that no one knows or understands. And worst of all, he is shouting at a kid! I can see everyone looking at him with surprised expressions on their faces. Some of those faces have even turned quite ugly as they stare at this mean man in the stands who has just berated a little boy in front of them.

When I suffered through this event those many years ago I thought that I was the only one hurt that day. Now I know differently. That man who stood up in the stands and yelled at his son in front of everybody—he is the one who suffered most. And he did it for me. It was for me that he allowed himself to be thought of as something far different than what he truly was. For me, he was willing to be thought of badly by others, though he was in fact the most kind and loving of fathers. For the sake of his little boy's arm, he was willing to sacrifice himself. I can only imagine now how the incredulous stares of the people that day must have wounded this genuinely sensitive and caring man. And it was all for love.

Our Lord himself has said, "There is no greater love than this, to lay down one's life for one's friends." As I remember that shout from the stands now, the words "Rod, NO!" no longer humiliate me. Instead, they create in me a very different kind of wound—the wound of love. And when I think of that spot in the stands once occupied by my father, I no longer see a big black "X" marking the spot where a man once lost his cool and embarrassed his son. Instead, as I see it now, that "X" has been transformed into a cross, a cross that is flowering and has turned that spot into the most beautiful one in the park. In the midst of sand and steel and stone, there is a little patch of loveliness surrounding that cross, marking the place where my father laid down his life for me. It was one of the many deaths, the painful humiliations, that my father has suffered willingly for love of me.

Now, as I remember that scene from my youth, it becomes a point of grace for me. It gives rise in me to feelings of deepest love and gratitude. It leads to prayers of contrition and thanksgiving. So often we go through life failing to recognize the great gifts of love that are given to us, gifts that echo the greatest of all loving gifts, and which can themselves become the inspiration for us to give such gifts ourselves. I am thankful that the Lord has opened my eyes to such things, at least a little. I am thankful that the Lord has given me a father who has in so many ways imaged for me the meaning of love. And I pray that at least in some small way I may follow his example.

Questions for Reflection

Can I remember a time when someone willingly suffered pain or humiliation for love of me?

Are there ways that I am suffering for love of another?

How does this connect me to the cross of Christ?

Crucified Lord, your willingness to suffer on my behalf is something that continually amazes me. May your love be so deeply rooted in me that I will find it possible to bear the cross for love of others.

❧ Why I'm a Vegetarian ❧

I KNOW it bothers some people that I'm a vegetarian. A guy who doesn't eat meat just doesn't seem natural to those who have grown up believing that if people weren't meant to eat meat then God wouldn't have given them teeth. Of course, there's no arguing with that kind of logic. Actually, I wouldn't want to. I'm not a vegetarian because I think everyone should be one. I don't know enough to be able to hold, much less support such an opinion.

I do know that from the standpoint of the stewardship of resources, we could feed more people more good food more easily if we didn't use so much of it to feed animals, which we then use to feed ourselves. In other words, it takes a lot more crops to fatten animals that are then used to fatten people than it does to just use the crops to fatten people in the first place. In terms of the stewardship of the earth's limited resources, then, being a vegetarian does make some sense.

Of course, if animals could talk they would probably give us another good reason for being vegetarians. Now maybe I'm wrong, but I just have to think that if animals could talk they would tell us that it just doesn't seem right that they can't live out the natural course of their days simply because we have a hankering for meat. Perhaps if we actually had to eat meat to live then at least some of the other creatures with whom we share the planet would grudgingly acknowledge the necessity of making a sacrifice for the sake of preserving humankind. But this is not the case. For us, eating meat is not a necessity.

If animals could talk, perhaps they also would tell us that they would willingly offer up their lives for us if we would just treat them a bit more humanely. By this they wouldn't mean that we should treat them like human beings, but that we should behave like human beings in our treatment of them. They might point out that for purposes of ease and profitability we have taken them out of their natural habitats and crowded them together by the hundreds or thousands to simply eat, breed, and die. And we want them to do it all as quickly as possible. Undoubtedly they would point out that while they may not be created in the image and likeness of God in the way that humans claim to be, they have been created by God nonetheless and are therefore deserving of being treated with a fair amount of dignity.

Of course I know that animals can't talk. And if they could, they might not say any of these things because, admittedly, I don't have the foggiest notion how animals think. But I can't help thinking that if they did think this way, they would have a point. And I find this point quite compelling. Actually, I have been sympathetic to this way of thinking for a long time. In fact, I was even inclined to this viewpoint during most of those years when I was still eating meat.

So why am I a vegetarian now? The answer is simple. I have a daughter named Ruth. And I love her. Ruth decided when she was in the fifth grade that the way we treat animals is wrong and that she would never eat meat again. This was a major decision for an eleven-year-old. So, since this daughter of mine had the courage to do what I had thought of doing for decades, I decided that the least I could do was to support her in her decision by becoming a vegetarian along with her. What I had been unwilling to do out of principle, I did for love.

Besides, the permanent decisions of fifth graders are seldom permanent. At least this is what I thought. But with Ruth I should have known better.

It is now eight years later. Ruth is still a vegetarian. And so am I. But now I am not just a vegetarian out of love for her. The amazing thing about love is that it is so fruitful. Love begets love. Somehow, in choosing not to eat meat out of love for Ruth I also have come to embrace the love she has for all living creatures. This is not to say that those who eat meat do not love all living creatures. But it is to say that it is good for some to show this love by not eating meat. For it keeps before us the end to which love is leading all creation.

The prophet Isaiah spoke of this when he said,

The wolf shall live with the lamb,
the leopard shall lie down with the kid,
the calf and the lion and the fatling together,
and a little child shall lead them.
The cow and the bear shall graze,
their young shall lie down together;
and the lion shall eat straw like the ox.
The nursing child shall play over the hole of the asp,
and the weaned child shall put its hand on the adder's den.
They will not hurt or destroy on all my holy mountain;
for the earth will be full of the knowledge of the Lord
as the waters cover the sea. (11:6-9)

This is why I am a vegetarian. I think it's good that there are some people in the world whose unusual behavior reminds the rest of us where we are heading as the people of God. This is so because it tells us something of how we have to live now to prepare for life in that land of promise. In this regard it takes all kinds. And vegetarians are one of those kinds. Isaiah said that a little child would lead them. She certainly has led me. Thanks, Ruth.

Questions for Reflection

Are there things that I find disturbing about our stewardship of creation?

How must I change to fit more perfectly into the picture of God's kingdom presented in the scriptures?

God of all creation, all that you make is good and to be cherished. Help me to more fully appreciate the world you have given us and to live in it reverently and peacefully.

"They're Going to Remove My Bowels?"

I AM often amazed by the amount of pain and difficulties some people experience in life through no fault of their own. Richard was such a person. In terms of the hardships this man had to face, it could honestly be said that Job had nothing on him.

Here are only a few of the things Richard had to endure. As a young man in his thirties, Richard had an aneurysm in the neck that burst and almost killed him. The recovery from this serious condition was long and difficult, but it was only the beginning. Some years later Richard was in a car accident. Several members of his family were in the car with him. He was the sole survivor of that terrible crash. He recovered from the injuries. The memories and the questions were not quite so easy to deal with. But he managed somehow.

Through his middle years there continued to be various difficulties of one sort or another, but nothing to match what he was to suffer in his later years. His wife developed some serious health problems. She had to have a leg amputated. Richard could no longer care for her at home; so together they moved into a nursing home. Actually, Richard needed to be there even more than his wife did. She was the picture of health compared to him. Well, this might be stretching it a bit, but not too much. He suffered from cancer, emphysema, and congestive heart failure, all of which led to one serious complication after another. Priests were called to the hospital on numerous occasions, when the staff was certain that he was about to breathe his last. But somehow, each time he managed to keep breathing and recovered sufficiently to return to his room at the nursing home.

One of those near brushes with death occurred at the time of his fiftieth wedding anniversary. Richard and his wife had planned to mark this event by renewing their wedding vows. They had spoken to the priest about it, and he was prepared to conduct a little ceremony for them at the nursing home. However, knowing Richard's history, it was not surprising that a few days before the intended celebration, he went into congestive heart failure once again. He was rushed to the hospital. And it appeared that this time Richard really was dying. His condition grew worse and worse until finally he was almost totally unresponsive. He seemed unable to move or speak.

The family decided there wasn't time to wait for the priest to come. Since one of Richard's sons is a Protestant minister and was on the scene, he agreed to begin the little ceremony before it was too late. So Richard's daughter leaned over and said to him, "Dad, they're going to renew your vows now." At this Richard, who hadn't even moved for a couple days, sat bolt upright and shouted, "They're going to remove my bowels?!"

After all he had been through, who could blame Richard for hearing things this way? And in a way, it's a good thing he did. For it seems that this bit of "mishearing" provided such a jolt to his system that things actually started working again. A few days later, he was back at the nursing home, and he was able to have that fiftieth anniversary celebration with his wife after all.

To me, the amazing thing about this man was not the many trials and tribulations he endured, though I have known no one who has suffered more. What truly amazed me about Richard was his great faith. In my many visits with him in the hospital, no matter how poorly he was feeling, he always received me gladly. He responded to my words with his own words of faith. He appreciated my prayers and blessings. And he was always most eager to receive the Eucharist. The more I learned of his life story, the more I came to marvel at this.

I have heard it said by many that they don't know how anyone can endure great hardships in life without faith in God. I understand what they are saying. The assurance of God's presence and love in the midst of suffering can provide consolation and hope. But when one suffers so much, how does one keep on believing that God is good and that God really wants to have something to do with us? How does one keep from wanting to "curse God and die"? At times, in the face of so much tragedy in life, it seems that faith in God could cause more consternation than consolation.

But it was not so for Richard. He continued to remain steadfast in his faith throughout. He continued to hold on to his belief that there was some reason his life had unfolded in the way it did. And while he certainly was never able to figure out what that reason might be, he continued to believe that God knew more than he did. Actually, Richard didn't spend much time trying to unravel the theological intricacies of things, like what God caused and what God didn't. He simply concluded that God wouldn't do or let anything happen that he couldn't use to accomplish his purposes. So this beleaguered but unbeaten man continued to trust that all would work out for the best in the end, because the best is what God wants for all his people. And since God is God, Richard believed that he could pull it off.

I have to say that I've heard plenty of theologizing over the years about suffering and the providence of God. Some of it has tested my faith and some has strengthened it. But none of it has helped me to grow in faith as much as the faithful witness of people like Richard.

Questions for Reflection

What people have I known that maintained great faith through much suffering?

Are there ways in which I have grown closer to God through times of suffering?

Ever-faithful God, you accompany us through the valley of suffering. Help us to grow in our awareness of your presence and to trust your good will for us, especially in the most painful experiences of life.

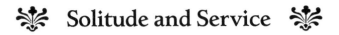 Solitude and Service

O UR own personal qualities and inclinations draw us toward certain saints as heroes, heroines, and role models. Since I am a reclusive sort by nature, I find myself most attracted to those who seem to have had a hankering for solitude. Among my favorites are Anthony of the Desert, Catherine of Siena, Julian of Norwich (whom I realize has not been canonized, but has been my own salvation on many occasions), and Teresa of Avila. Solitude had an important part to play in the lives of each one— the solitude of the cave, the room, the anchorhold, or the cell. Yet interestingly enough, and what I find most challenging, is that their solitude, though lengthy and extreme at times, was genera- tive of some kind of service to others that was dynamic and remarkably fruitful. Christianity has often been charged with being an escapist religion, especially those branches of it that focus on the importance of solitude. But there was nothing escapist about any of the four I have mentioned.

Anthony lived in Egypt during the third and fourth centuries. As a young man he was greatly moved by the gospel that says, "If you would be perfect, go sell what you have, give to the poor and come, follow me." So, over the course of time, this is what Anthony did, finally following the Lord to a cave in the Egyptian desert where he lived alone for twenty years. Needless to say, some people were worried about him. And the longer he stayed holed up in that cave, the more worried they became. While they were willing to admit that a little solitude might be a good thing, they were afraid that this was overkill. They were certain that being alone for such a long time would drive Anthony crazy. But much to their surprise, after twenty years of getting to know the Lord in the solitude of his cave, Anthony emerged as the picture of health. In fact, he seemed more radiant, more hospitable, more charming, more cheerful, and more eloquent than he ever had been.

Now with such good results, one might think that Anthony would have just remained there for the rest of his life. But after those twenty years alone with the Lord, it seems he was driven at times to leave his place of solitude and do something for someone. From time to time he would travel around the region visiting others who had come to live in the desert to do what he had done. He would offer them counsel. And he would encourage them to hang in there, for as attractive as it might have been to some initially, such a life was no picnic in the park. His holy cheerfulness brightened the caves of many and helped them to persevere.

But the most surprising thing of all was when Anthony left the desert to make the long journey to Alexandria where a great persecution of Christians was being waged by the emperor Maximus. He went there to lend his support to the community of the faithful, and to be martyred for the faith if necessary. Yet, he radiated such holiness, such courage and virtue, that the persecutors wouldn't touch him. His dynamic presence enabled many a Christian to hold fast until the crisis was averted. Only then did Anthony head back to his desert cave.

In a way Catherine of Siena's story is very different, yet in some ways it is remarkably the same. Catherine lived in Italy during the fourteenth century. As a young woman, she determined not to marry, but to give her life entirely to Christ. This was not something her parents were eager to hear, since Catherine was the youngest of twenty-five children. They were hoping to get a little something from marrying her off to help compensate for the expense of raising such an army of children. Yet Catherine was headstrong, or perhaps in this case one might say "head-shorn." At the age of fifteen she cut off her hair to make herself unattractive to men. And after one last attempt to convince her otherwise, her parents finally got the idea that she meant business.

So wisely, they gave in to Catherine's wishes. They let her have a little room to herself. And she stayed in that room for three years, never leaving it except to go to church. This was her place of solitude. It was a place in which she had many deep encounters with the Lord. At the end of those three years, she had the deepest encounter of all, an experience that is sometimes called the mystical marriage. In a vision Christ placed a band around her finger, taking her as his spouse, and promising to be with her to help her always.

You might imagine that such an experience would have left Catherine quite content to remain in that room with Christ forever. Actually, it did. But to her dismay, the Lord himself told her that she must leave that room. If she wanted to be with him always, she would have to go out from her room and be with those most in need, for that is where he would be. So Catherine left her place of solitude and took up one of the most incredibly active lives of service the world has ever known. She cared for the sick, especially the ones in such frightful condition that nobody else would have anything to do with them. She visited prisoners, tended to the dying, was called in to settle disputes between various city-states in Italy, corresponded with kings and queens, and even became an advisor to the pope. And she accomplished all this before she died at the tender age of thirty-three.

A contemporary of Catherine's, Julian of Norwich lived during the fourteenth century in England. She is what was called an anchoress, mainly because she lived in something called an anchorhold. An anchorhold was a room attached to the side of a church, with one window looking into the church and another looking out to the world. An anchoress was enclosed in this room for her entire life, living a life of prayer and solitude.

In her anchorhold, Julian had plenty of time to reflect on an experience she had as a young woman. She had become seriously ill, so ill that everyone thought she was dying, including her. The priest was called; he came and held a crucifix before her. As she gazed on that crucifix, she had a vision. It was a vision of Christ actually suffering upon the cross. Through this vision of his agony, Christ revealed his great love for her and for all humankind. While Julian wrote the vision down, she continued to reflect upon it for the next twenty years. It had a profound influence on her life.

Often people would stop by and speak with her through the window in her anchorhold, seeking counsel from this holy woman who had had such an intimate encounter with God. She responded to them kindly, assuring them of God's loving ways. In addition to the spiritual counsel given gladly to those who visited her, after those twenty years of reflection on her loving encounter with Christ, she wrote of it again. She explained more fully the love of God as she had come to know it, in hopes that others might be helped by it. Though she never left the anchorhold, she too reached out from her place of solitude in ways that would be helpful to others.

Moving on to Teresa of Avila, who lived in Spain in the sixteenth century, we find that while her situation in life was a bit different from Anthony, Catherine or Julian, the dynamic of solitude leading to service was quite the same. Teresa became a Carmelite nun at a fairly young age. However, it took her quite a while to become totally comfortable with solitude. It seems that Teresa liked to talk. She enjoyed receiving people in the convent's parlor and chatting about what was going on in the world. After about twenty years of this, she finally got down to business and made her cell a true place of prayerful solitude, where she devoted herself entirely to developing her relationship with Christ. Now in her forties, she began to have many profound mystical experiences which totally "mystified" some of her confessors, who knew all too well of her history of socializing at the expense of praying. Yet she continued to receive constant visions of Christ, leading up to her own experience of the mystical marriage.

Again, one would think that after such an experience, Teresa would have been content to remain in her cell for the rest of her life. But instead, she became so fired up about helping others in her order to experience the kind of spiritual awakening she had, that, along with St. John of the Cross, she led a reform of her entire order, founding new convents in many parts of Spain. She also wrote many books about the spiritual life. In the most famous of her writings, *The Interior Castle,* Teresa describes the stages of spiritual growth and what her readers might experience at each stage so they wouldn't be frightened by some of the strange things that might happen to them.

Yet, Teresa makes it very clear where such experience must lead, if it is truly genuine. Toward the end of her book, where she describes the final stage of spiritual growth, she says something that might seem surprising to those who know nothing of the Christian tradition of solitude. She says that there comes a point where the more sensational experiences of private encounter with God diminish in frequency and intensity. This happens so that the person who has been transformed through powerful encounters with the Lord may engage more fully in Christian service. Ultimately, she says, the Christian life must be a blending of solitude and service. Or, putting an interesting twist on a beloved gospel story, she says that there must be a merging of Martha and Mary. Clearly Teresa got it right. This essential relationship between solitude and service is reflected in the lives of all the saints, flowing from the very life of Christ himself, who came not to be served but to serve, and to give his life as a ransom for the many. For the Christian, solitude is never an end in itself. It is always linked to service.

Though I am certainly not in a class with any of the spiritual heroes I have mentioned here, this truth they taught so well is one that resonates deeply with my own limited experience. Long ago now, the summer before my senior year in high school, I had heard a bit about God and prayer from one of my friends. Having had no previous experience in the religious realm (at least in terms of my own awareness), I decided to check it out. Lord knows I needed something! So after spending an evening alone in my room, mostly feeling sorry for myself, I decided to give the prayer thing a try. I got down on my knees by the side of my bed and prayed, "If there is a God, I want to know about it." Suddenly I was enveloped by a loving presence, a presence so wonderful that it wiped away all the fears and misgivings I had about life. In its place was left the deepest joy and peace I had ever known.

"Wow," you might say, "I'll bet you could have stayed there in your room lingering over that experience forever." This would be a good guess, but entirely wrong. Instead, like Anthony, Catherine, Julian, and Teresa, along with the experience of God that took place in the solitude of my room, I was left with a profound sense that I was to devote my life to serving God's church in some way, though to this point, I had never been involved with a church at all.

From the very first moment of my life as a Christian, solitude and service were joined. Of course, the challenge is to maintain the right balance for a lifetime. For me the temptation is to seek solitude as an escape from service. For others the temptation is to engage in service as a way of avoiding solitude. But, if we would be perfect, as Christ is perfect, the two must be joined. That's why I ask Anthony, Catherine, Julian, and Teresa to pray for me on a regular basis!

Questions for Reflection

How are solitude and service balanced in my life?

Who are the models of the life of solitude and service that are most important to me?

God of awesome integrity, you call us to reach out to others as you reach out to us, balancing solitude and service. Help us to remain faithful to both these important aspects of the life we share in Christ.

❧ A Lasting Legacy ❧

THE last time I was with a Methodist Congregation for worship was about fifteen years ago, when the last parish I served as a Methodist minister invited me back to preach at the celebration of their centennial. This was four years after I had left them to become a Roman Catholic. The fact that they invited me back at all certainly says something about the kind of people they are. The love they showed me as I journeyed forth with my family on what for them must have seemed a very strange pathway indeed is something that I will never forget.

Nor will I forget the lessons I learned from the founder of all Methodist congregations, a priest by the name of John Wesley. As a seminarian and then as a young minister, I spent a good bit of time studying Wesley's life and writings. The story of his life is a legacy I received from my time with the Methodists which has continued to be of great value to me. In fact, in a way it has come to mean even more to me now than it did when I was a young Methodist clergyman, for now I am in a much better position to understand it and receive its most profound gifts.

One part of Wesley's story that has come alive for me in recent years has to do with his experience as a young Anglican priest-missionary on assignment to the United States. It was in the mid-eighteenth century. John Wesley and a few of his Methodist friends agreed to go to the colony of Georgia, to make real Christians out of the settlers there and to convert the Indians. They had come to be called Methodists because of their strict, methodical discipline. They rose early every morning to begin a very structured day of prayer, Scripture reading, study, liturgical celebration, and pastoral work. It was their notion that this is what it means to be a truly dedicated Christian. Unfortunately, most of the colonists in Georgia were of a mind that they were already dedicated Christians, without all the "extras" that Wesley was trying to foist on them as necessary Christian practice. They didn't take kindly to his "holier than thou" attitude and his constant pious harassment of them.

To make matters worse, John Wesley got caught up in an affair of the heart. Along with the other missionaries, Wesley had vowed to have no romantic involvements during their time in America. But the strength of that promise was not enough to keep him from falling madly in love with a young woman named Sophie Hopkey. He was terribly smitten. However, though he courted her right along for quite some time, he could never bring himself to pop the question. Perhaps he felt this would have been too great a betrayal of his friends. All we know for sure is that after waiting as long as she could on a proposal from the Reverend Mr. Wesley, and with the prospect of becoming an old maid staring her in the face, Sophie agreed to marry another. Wesley was so heartbroken by the whole thing that he barred Sophie from Communion, on the grounds that she had been dishonest with him about the matters of her heart. Of course, the real problem was that he had been unable to deal honestly with the matters of his own heart.

Sophie's father happened to be a prominent citizen. So Wesley's barring of his ex-girlfriend from Communion was something that couldn't be done quietly. The townspeople were incensed. They could recognize a travesty of justice when they saw it. The lynch-party was on its way to administer swift justice when Wesley caught wind of it and ran for his life. He hopped on the first boat he could find to make his way back to England.

It should be no surprise that this devastating experience in Georgia sent John Wesley into a severe depression. It had called into question everything he believed in so deeply. Even worse, it revealed to him some of the flaws in his own character that he had been unwilling to face. He felt he had let everyone down and that he had no business being a priest. This man who once thought he knew it all and was willing to promote what he knew with great zeal, suddenly felt as though he knew nothing, and, even worse, that he was nothing. The wind had definitely been taken out of his sails. And for him, like anyone else, who has plummeted into the dark valley of depression, death seemed the most attractive of all future possibilities.

Fortunately, there was a Moravian minister on board that ship, who was a very wise and holy man. When Wesley told him of the shattered state of his existence and asked, "How can I preach the faith when I find I have none myself?" he received some simple but extraordinary counsel. "Preach faith until you have it." This was the word the minister passed on to him from the one who is the origin of all such saving words.

"Preach faith until you have it." It was another way of saying that there is life on the other side of depression, regardless of how it might seem at the moment. The truth you once saw so clearly doesn't cease to exist when you are in the darkness of depression any more than the sun ceases to exist when it goes behind a cloud. And the possibility of your working as a servant of the truth is not extinguished because the fire has gone out. As long as there continues to be the slightest spark, the tiniest of glowing embers, there is always the possibility that the fire will be whipped up again. Though you can't see it now, you must listen to those who know that there is life on the other side of depression, because they have been through this valley themselves. John Wesley accepted this wise counsel. And, as hard as it was, he kept on doing the best he could until the life fires began to whip up again.

This part of Wesley's story had always fascinated me, though for reasons that were not exactly clear, until a few years ago when I found myself in that dark valley of depression. How I got to that place of lifelessness is not quite as clear as it was in Wesley's case. No major events or situations were the obvious trigger that catapulted me over the edge. Actually, I had been moving toward that valley for a long time, but wasn't willing to admit it or do anything about it until it was too late. Then, in terms of loss of vitality and inner anguish, I found myself precisely where Wesley had been during that lonely boat ride home.

Here is one thing I wrote while wallowing in that valley of darkness. (Please note that this is a journal entry and not a polished poem.)

> I am in the dark valley now,
> Perhaps deeper than I have ever gone,
> Into the valley of death
> Where the silence of despair
> Is only broken by weeping and sighs.
>
> Trembling seizes one there
> At the slightest of disturbances,
> Where the least burden
> Is transformed into a millstone
> And the unpleasant thought shoots out spasms of pain.
>
> In this valley of darkness
> The face goes dead

And the body becomes an immovable object
Waiting for a spark of light and warmth
To set the energy flowing once again.

In this place there is no prayer
Except the intercessions
Continuing in the deep places, unknown but real,
And the cry of abandonment
Which mysteriously ties us to the Lord.

In recounting my own personal experience and remembering that of John Wesley I realized that, though I may have left his church, we were still soul mates nonetheless. And I discovered that the counsel he received, about continuing to preach faith until he had it, was still solid. When you are in the valley of depression, it is not the time to start off on a different path, because you can't see clearly enough to know where you are, or where that other path might be going. Keep traveling the road until you can begin to see again. Keep speaking the words of life and truth you once knew until you are in a position to know them again. This is what John Wesley did. And in so doing, he proved to be a good guide for me.

When John Wesley finally made his way out of the dark valley with God's help, there was life again. In fact, there was a far greater depth and vibrancy to his life on the other side of depression than there had been before. As I have reflected on his story, it has become clear to me that there would have been no Methodist revival in England, and later in the United States, if Wesley hadn't lived through his depressive ordeal. Before this, he was a rather stuffy cleric who was unwilling to depart from established practice, except to make his own disciplines, and those of others, more severe.

Except for the great depression he had suffered through, I doubt if he would have ever responded to the request to begin preaching in the fields to the poor who were alienated from a church that seemed to cater only to the wealthy. Wesley was moved to reach out to them. And people came to hear him by the thousands.

When Wesley first took up this field preaching it is said that he looked like a statue, the only thing that moved was his mouth. After all, he had been trained for preaching in a very formal setting. But people were so in need of the good news he had to proclaim to them, that, regardless of the style of presentation, large numbers of those who heard him were swooning, being slain in the Spirit, and finding themselves converted to a new way of life right there on the spot.

Again, Wesley's story speaks to me. It's not that I have suddenly taken to the streets and to the countryside, preaching the good news to thousands. But I do find myself much more ready to minister to hurting people, and with a new depth of compassion. And I am willing to try new ways of ministering to others, and even new ways of living life, that go beyond what I would have been open to before my own very slow excursion through the valley of depression.

My own intention is not to become the founder of a church, or even to lead a religious revival. I simply want to become a better husband, father, neighbor and priest. And I find hope in Wesley's story that such a thing is possible. Among many others, this is an enduring gift that I have received from my time among the Methodists. Though I am no longer part of Wesley's fold, he and his people continue to hold a special place in my heart.

Questions for Reflection

Have there been times when you felt too discouraged to continue on?

What helped you to get back on your feet?

How could you help someone else to get back on theirs?

Compassionate God, lift me up when I am down. And plant in me the gentle urge to help others get back on their feet.

A Tribute to Brother Francis

SINCE much of the writing for this volume has been done at the Franciscan Renewal Center in Tiffin, Ohio, I think it is only fitting to include a little reflection on St. Francis. His influence permeates this place and all who come here. Everywhere you turn there is a picture, icon, statue or wood carving of St. Francis. In the library there are numerous volumes and videos on his life and spirituality. But even without these obvious reminders, one could easily guess who is the underlying inspiration of this physical and spiritual oasis. There is a wonderful simplicity to the building and to the people who staff it, reflecting the holy poverty that Francis promoted ceaselessly.

The grounds are well cared for, with beautiful gardens containing flowers, fruits and vegetables of every sort. Bordering these lands tended by the Tiffin Franciscans are lush fields of corn and soybeans. Birds are present in abundance, along with squirrels, rabbits, frogs, muskrats, and other little creatures that live along the creek that runs through the property. Here it is only necessary to open one's eyes to catch a glimpse of the goodness of creation, the interrelatedness of all things, and the love for all creatures that Francis promoted with great gusto.

One can also sense here a kind of earthiness, a grounding in what is, without the need or inclination to put on airs. This is something that typified the life of Brother Francis, as he liked to be called. Here people are who they are. Nobody is out to wow you. The meals are plentiful and hearty, but not fancy. Flowers from the garden adorn the tables. One can see nuns' underwear flapping on the clothesline, and nobody thinks anything of it.

Something else evident here is a commitment to serving those in need. On the grounds is a nursing home, including a hospice and a rehabilitation center. The retreat house itself makes its space available for a county program intended to help those who have been convicted of drunk driving. A weekly meeting of Seneca County's AIDS Task Force is held here. In addition, the proceeds from the gift shop benefit organizations serving the poor, or the poor craftspersons themselves. The whole environment in which all this happens is filled with reminders both visual and verbal that all that is done for the needy here flows from the love of Christ, something that Francis believed in very much.

As one would expect of a community founded under the patronage of St. Francis, love for the Church, for prayer, and most especially for the Eucharist is the underlying foundation of all that happens here. This daily communal prayer flows into the constant private prayer that permeates and flavors everything. Rosary beads in an elderly sister's hand, quick glances heavenward, lips moving quietly, candles burning, all hint at the unseen power that gives life to those who live and work here. The spirit of Brother Francis is manifested mightily in this place.

However, one of the things I have noticed during my stay, which did not typify the life of St. Francis, is a healthy concern for the body. At the Renewal Center there is an office of natural medicine, which takes a wholistic approach in assisting people to overcome bodily ailments. Programs are offered here that focus on healthy eating and healthy living. Courses are offered on yoga and relaxation techniques. One can even arrange for a therapeutic massage.

I am glad to see this dedication to promoting physical health along with the spiritual, though it is well known that this is not something Francis practiced in his own life. Instead, Francis was known for his great physical austerities, even for punishing his body with severe disciplines. Yet, I do believe that the concern for the body promoted by the Tiffin Franciscans also flows from the influence of Brother Francis, but in a most unusual way.

Actually, its genesis lies in a very obscure story from late in Francis' life. Of course, multitudes of interesting stories flow from his life. Quite a few of them are well known. Many have heard of his experience at San Damiano, where, while praying before the cross, he received a message from the Lord to repair his church, which was falling down all around him. Most have heard of Francis preaching to birds and other various kinds of critters. Some have surely heard of his initiation of the Christmas creche. And almost everyone knows that he received the stigmata.

However, there is one story that most people do not know. For some reason, it has always fascinated me. I find it to be one of the most moving and compelling scenes from the life of this great saint. It occurred toward the end of his life. His body had deteriorated badly. He was in constant pain; could hardly see; needed help to walk or to do almost anything. Francis realized that much of this was the result of his terribly harsh treatment of his body over the years.

Through most of his life, Francis had been caught up in a very sharp body/spirit dualism, something rather common among medieval mystics. As he saw it, the spiritual aspect of a person was of singular importance. The goal of life was to save one's soul. So it was the soul that was to be cultivated, while the body was of no real consequence. This is why Francis punished his body whenever it seemed to take his attention away from spiritual things. He disciplined it as one would an unruly animal. He treated it as nothing more than a beast of burden that carried the soul during one's earthly life and enabled one to engage in those physical tasks necessary to assist one's neighbor, which was an absolute necessity for spiritual growth. It is no accident, then, that Francis had often referred to his body as "Brother Ass."

However, as the story goes, toward the end of his life, Francis came to see things differently. He realized that his diminished capacity to work and to minister to people's needs was the direct result of the abuse of his body. And so he apologized to his body for having treated it so cruelly. In the end, he came to see that there is an integral relationship between the physical and spiritual. If one is to truly serve the poor in imitation of Christ, then a healthy body helps. And a healthy body can do the most good when it is animated by a well-formed spirit. Ultimately Francis came to see that the body, as a gift of God's creation, is not to be neglected or treated badly, for it too is a reflection of the divine goodness.

I, for one, am very glad that Brother Francis came to this important realization before he died. It has certainly made my month's stay at the Renewal Center much more pleasurable than it might have been otherwise. The food has been good and plentiful each day. The cook has taken great care to cover all the nutritional bases, which has been a bit more challenging than usual because I am a vegetarian. Also, a special place was found in the building where I could keep my bicycle. And the staff enthusiastically supported my desire to pedal out into the countryside for some vigorous exercise each day. In my suite, I have been provided with a comfortable bed and enough space to move about and to stretch out from time to time. I have even been blessed with an air conditioner! I'm sure St. Francis never would have used such a thing, not even at the end of his life when he came to see things differently. It takes a little while to make concrete adjustments after one experiences a change of heart. Thankfully, someone remembered this little part of Brother Francis' story. And I'm happy to have reaped some of the benefits!

Questions for Reflection

Is there a healthy balance to my life in terms of physical and spiritual exercise?

How am I tending to my own needs as I tend to the needs of others?

God of all creation, help me to respect and nurture the gift of my own life that I may honor the good you have done in creating me while striving to help others make the most of the life you have given them.

❧ In Memory of Her ❧

MOST of those who perform great acts of love become nameless figures in the annals of history. But their deeds of love remain. The deeds are not so easily forgotten as the names. In my lifetime I have heard hundreds of stories about great acts of love, told to me by eyewitnesses.

I once heard of a man who donated one of his kidneys to his brother. But I don't remember the man's name. I was told of a woman who gave up a lucrative business position to become the full-time caregiver for her ailing mother. But I couldn't tell you her name either. Then there was the little girl who placed her favorite doll in the toy bin for poor little children who have nothing. Her name has long since vanished from my memory, but not her act of love. In a sense, this is the way it should be since true acts of love are always selfless. People don't do them so that someone will remember their name. They do them because something deep within tells them they must. The gift of love itself is what's important, not the fact that they are recognized for it.

This is beautifully reflected in a little story toward the end of the gospel of Mark. It happened just a couple days before Passover, when Jesus would suffer his terrible death upon the cross. Of course, nobody knew what would soon be happening to the Lord except, perhaps, for an unknown woman who had a deep love for him. It may be that she had some special intuition of what was about to happen. We don't know for sure. What we do know is that she came into the house of Simon the leper, where Jesus was sitting at table. She went up to him, broke open a jar of very costly ointment, and poured it on his head. Some were disturbed by this action. It seemed frivolous. The ointment could have been sold for a good bit of money, which could have been used to assist the poor.

Of course, Jesus knew what no one else in that room could possibly know except, perhaps, the woman herself. This loving action was a preparation for his death, an anointing for his burial. But perhaps even more, he knew that this was a great act of love, one that would help to sustain him during the ordeal he was to soon endure. His remembering of this remarkably loving action would help to see him through the darkness of that day, bolstering his trust that love would be waiting for him on the other side of death. So he openly expressed his gratitude for the good thing that she had done for him. Then, he said, quite remarkably, that from that time forward, wherever the good news was proclaimed in all the world, what she had done would be told in memory of her.

So it has. This woman's loving deed has become a part of the gospel story that has been told throughout the world, now for some two thousand years. Yet, as with the doers of so many great acts of love, her name is not what has been remembered, but only the act itself. This seems fitting, because it is not her name but her loving deed that continues to enrich human life after all these years. And this is probably just the way she wanted it.

I'm sure this was true for another obscure woman who also performed some great acts of love—my mother. She was a fairly reclusive woman during my growing up years. Such tendencies seem to run strong in her bloodline. Mom spent most of her time in the house. She seemed to be rather frightened of social contacts. Though she was a very good and intelligent woman, she never seemed to think much of herself. She didn't want to subject herself to the scrutiny of others, lest they find in her some imperfection. Instead, she preferred to stay in the safe environment of her own house with those she knew loved and appreciated her.

The world's loss was our gain. Mom was a very loving and compassionate woman. And because she spent most of her time at home, my sister and I were the most frequent recipients of her loving actions. She would read to us for hours. She would read the same books over and over again at our request, until we knew the stories by heart. (It wasn't until I had children of my own and began reading to them myself that I realized what a great labor of love this was.) She held us close to her when we were hurting. She called the doctor when we were sick, which was itself a labor of love, since she seemed to have a great fear of calling people on the phone. She even called for the taxi and would go with us to the doctor's office so our father could stay at work. She stood by us and supported us through all of life's crises. I can't think of a single instant when I doubted that she loved me with all her heart.

When my father retired, he and mom moved to Florida. They lived in one of those mobile home communities where everyone knows their neighbors and becomes something of a large family. It was the best thing that ever happened to her. There she found the security and support she needed to share herself with others. Unfortunately, after a few years mom developed cancer. She fought the disease boldly, going through several rounds of chemotherapy, which were in many ways worse than the cancer itself. However, difficult as it was, she never complained about her illness. My guess is that she was always much worse off than she ever let us know because she didn't want to burden us in any way. Finally, realizing that her end was near, mom and dad went to stay with my sister Debbie, who is a nurse and could provide good care for her. This brings me to the story of her greatest act of love.

Mom knew that my family was going to come to see her at Thanksgiving time. If we would have known how ill she was, we would have come much sooner. But it seems she didn't want to make us change our plans. Instead, she waited for us. How she continued to hang on is one of those great mysteries of life. After seeing how weak she was and how difficult it was for her to breathe, I am convinced that she simply fought off death by the sheer strength of her will until we arrived. This was her final act of love. She continued to suffer willingly so that we would be able to see each other one more time. She courageously resisted death until we arrived so that we would know of her great love for us. It was only a few hours after we got there that mom died, with my sister and me at her side.

By the way, my mother's name is Madalyn. I know you won't remember it. It's not important. What is important is that her great act of love be remembered. So if you ever tell my story to anyone, I hope you will tell what she did for me, in memory of her. I know I will.

Questions for Reflection

What great act of love has another done for me?

What have I done to remember and to celebrate that person's life?

Loving God, you have sent many people into my life who have shared wondrous gifts of love for me. Help me to remember these precious people and to imitate them in reaching out in love to others.

POSTSCRIPT

❧ "What Are You Doing ❧ Here?"

"**W**HAT are you doing here, Elijah?" Elijah recognized the voice. Actually, it wasn't really a voice. It was no more than a faint whispering sound. In fact, it wasn't even a sound. Elijah had often encountered this voice, not as noise heard with the ears but as a nagging sense that came upon him when he least expected it. It was a wordless word that produced in him an awareness that God wanted something of him, or that God wanted something for him. With God there really wasn't any difference. Everything God had ever wanted of him had also been for him, though sometimes it had taken awhile for him to realize it. Elijah knew as well as anyone the truth of what Paul was to articulate so beautifully centuries later, that, "in all things God works for good for those who love him and are called according to his purpose."

The prophet saw this quite clearly when he stood on Mt. Carmel basking in the brilliant blaze God had unleashed in answer to his prayers, while the prophets of Baal stood by dumbfounded. They had been unable to raise even a puff of smoke with their most potent petitions. Following the rout on the mountaintop, Elijah continued to be aware of the powerful presence of God as with the blade of his knife he quickly dispatched each one of those pagan prophets to wherever it is in the next world that pagan prophets go.

However, all that had been so clear to Elijah about the presence and purpose of God quickly vanished when Queen Jezebel vowed to do to him what he had done to those prophets of hers. He had seen what the queen had done to others who had caused her much less embarrassment than this. And this frightful vision supplanted the one he had seen on the top of Mt. Carmel. Elijah panicked. He ran. No, it was not his usual way of responding to tough situations. But such things do happen, even to those with faith of legendary proportions.

Yet God did not abandon Elijah, even in his flight of fright. Angels were sent with food and drink to sustain him in his running, until finally he collapsed into a cave on Mt. Horeb. It was there that he heard the divine voice. "What are you doing here Elijah?"

That Elijah heard the divine voice in this particular place asking this particular question is really no surprise. It would have happened even if Horeb hadn't been known as the mountain of God. Whenever a person stops running and comes to a place of silence the divine voice can be heard asking, "What are you doing here?" Of course, God already knows the answer. Yet God asks the question anyway because we need to know the answer too. It was certainly a life-saver for Elijah. For in answering this question Elijah heard himself speak the truth of his life. "I have been very zealous for the Lord, the God of hosts; for the Israelites have forsaken your covenant, thrown down your altars, and killed your prophets with the sword. I alone am left, and they are seeking my life, to take it away." For the first time in many days, Elijah heard himself speak the truth of his love for God, of his concern for his people, of his loneliness, and of his fears. This is what often happens in those silent stopping places of life.

The articulation of one's response to the divine question, "What are you doing here?" inevitably leads to the raising of the complementary human question, "What are You doing here?" In the silence of those private places where the divine voice is heard one can't help but wonder what God is doing there. "Why are You still with me?" "What are You trying to tell me?" "What are You asking of me?" "How can You help me?" "Can I really trust You?" These are all variations of the basic question of God's presence and activity.

What Elijah was doing in that cave on Mt. Horeb is what we might call spiritual reflection. No amount of book learning or formal religious instruction can take the place of this important work, though it can certainly help to prepare for it. In fact, the study of the Christian faith will confront us with the conviction that our destiny is determined by the actual living of life and by our relationship with the God who gives it. So it is essential to put ourselves in a position where we will hear God speak to us the question, "What are you doing here?" But this does little good unless we are also willing to take the time necessary to answer God's question, to ask our own questions of God, and to listen for a response. This is what I'm talking about when I speak of spiritual reflection.

The essays I have shared in this book are the result of doing spiritual reflection on the stuff of my life. They are the result of spending time in my own personal "cave places" where God has broken through the silence with the question "What are you doing here?" Sometimes when God broaches this question I have to admit that I really don't know. Then, out of the silence a memory may emerge. It's as if God is saying, "Remember when this happened? It is part of what has brought you here. Let's think together about what it means." At other times I will be very much aware of what I am doing in that "cave place." Something has happened that has had an immediate and profound effect on me. Again, out of the silence God will suggest that we explore its meaning together. During this reflection things will come to mind – sayings that I've heard, things I've learned through study over the years, certain bits of Scripture I've read, or some experience I've had.

Somehow, as I chew over these things in the presence of God, some insight into life emerges. Remarkably, such things as awkward moments in the life of a married priest, a grandmother's breaking of wind, the gift of a dollar, a sip of whiskey given to a three-year-old, lessons from people who lived long ago, a mother's parting gift, have become bearers of divine revelations. The process is mysterious and unpredictable. But the fruits are indeed delicious.

I have enjoyed collecting these fruits and presenting them to you in this volume. I hope you have enjoyed tasting them. My further hope is that by now you have come to realize that there is always a ready supply of such fruits available to you. And you needn't even buy another book! All you need to do is take up the practice of spiritual reflection yourself.

Other Titles You Might Enjoy

GRACE NOTES
Embracing the Joy of Christ in a Broken World
Lorraine V. Murray

". . . wlll help you to see what we should be able to see naturally, but for some reason it takes grace to recognize grace! Her book is well named." **—Fr. Richard Rohr, O.F.M.**

"A book for seekers who want to recover their childhood faith on an adult level." **—Brother David Steindl-Rast, OSB**

No. RP 154/04 ISBN 1-878718-69-X   **$9.95**

MOTHER O' MINE: A Legacy of Remembrance
Harry W. Paige

Rich in imagery, history and spirituality, these stories evoke the nearness of those we have loved—beyond the graves that hold them. A perfect gift for anyone who has or desires a deep and abiding love for their mother.

"Harry Paige has been a favorite of Catholic Digest readers for more than four decades. This evocative collection in honor of his mother makes it easy to see why."
—Richard Reece, Editor

No. RP 182/04 ISBN 1-878718-81-9   **$9.95**

FEASTS OF LIFE
Recipes from Nana's Wooden Spoon
Father Jim Vlaun

"Filled with wonderful stories and even better-sounding recipes in seven categories . . . The dishes are easy to make and don't require fancy ingredients—just good, old-fashioned meats, cheese and vegetables. . . . Includes a prayer for grace, a cooking equivalents table and a cross-referenced index." **—Crux of the News**

No. RP 168/04 ISBN 1-878718-76-2   **$12.95**

THE POWER OF ONE
Christian Living in the Third Millennium
Msgr. Jim Lisante

The latest collection of his award-winning columns contains an entire section devoted to the emotional and spiritual recovery from September 11, 2001. As always there is much to inform, challenge and inspire all ages and stages of faith. Discover how ordinary folks and well known actors, authors and clergy are transforming the world through word and action

No . RP180/04 ISBN 1-878718-84-3   **$9.95**

www.catholicbookpublishing.com

Other Titles by the Author

THE JOY OF PREACHING:
Embracing the Gift and the Promise
Rev. Rod Damico

The author offers preachers of all denominations a wealth of material, often amusing and always practical. He invites readers to deeply embrace both the painful sacrifice and exquisite joy of the call to speak of what they love.

"Joy is the thread that holds this book together. . . . the joy of speaking of what we love to whom we love."
—From the Foreword by Walter J. Burghardt, S.J.

No. RP 142/04 ISBN 1-878718-61-4   **$6.95**

THE JOY OF WORSHIPING TOGETHER
Giving and Getting the Most from Mass
Father Rod Damico

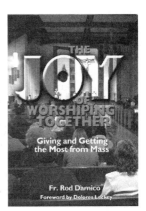

". . . creates a most graceful bridge between two authentic expressions of Church: the domestic church (the church of the home) and the gathered church (the parish). . . . traversing this bridge leads one to a richer understanding of the worshiping community. More than that, it leads one deeper into the Mystery of God."

—From the Foreword by Dolores Leckey

No. RP 166/04 ISBN 1-878718-74-6   **$5.95**

www.catholicbookpublishing.com

Additional Titles Published by Resurrection Press, a Catholic Book Publishing Imprint

A Rachel Rosary *Larry Kupferman*	$4.50
A Season in the South *Marci Alborghetti*	$10.95
Blessings All Around *Dolores Leckey*	$8.95
Catholic Is Wonderful *Mitch Finley*	$4.95
Come, Celebrate Jesus! *Francis X. Gaeta*	$4.95
Days of Intense Emotion *Keeler/Moses*	$12.95
Discernment *Chris Aridas*	$8.95
From Holy Hour to Happy Hour *Francis X. Gaeta*	$7.95
Grace Notes *Lorraine Murray*	$9.95
Healing through the Mass *Robert DeGrandis, SSJ*	$9.95
Our Grounds for Hope *Fulton J. Sheen*	$7.95
The Healing Rosary *Mike D.*	$5.95
Healing Your Grief *Ruthann Williams, OP*	$7.95
Heart Peace *Adolfo Quezada*	$9.95
Life, Love and Laughter *Jim Vlaun*	$7.95
The Joy of Being an Altar Server *Joseph Champlin*	$5.95
The Joy of Being a Catechist *Gloria Durka*	$4.95
The Joy of Being a Eucharistic Minister *Mitch Finley*	$5.95
The Joy of Being a Lector *Mitch Finley*	$5.95
The Joy of Being an Usher *Gretchen Hailer, RSHM*	$5.95
The Joy of Marriage Preparation *McDonough/Marinelli*	$5.95
The Joy of Music Ministry *J.M. Talbot*	$6.95
The Joy of Praying the Rosary *James McNamara*	$5.95
The Joy of Teaching *Joanmarie Smith*	$5.95
Lights in the Darkness *Ave Clark, O.P.*	$8.95
Loving Yourself for God's Sake *Adolfo Quezada*	$5.95
Meditations for Survivors of Suicide *Joni Woelfel*	$8.95
Mother Teresa *Eugene Palumbo, S.D.B.*	$5.95
Mourning Sickness *Keith Smith*	$8.95
Personally Speaking *Jim Lisante*	$8.95
Practicing the Prayer of Presence *Muto/van Kaam*	$8.95
Prayers from a Seasoned Heart *Joanne Decker*	$8.95
Praying the Lord's Prayer with Mary *Muto/vanKaam*	$8.95
5-Minute Miracles *Linda Schubert*	$4.95
Sabbath Moments *Adolfo Quezada*	$6.95
Season of New Beginnings *Mitch Finley*	$4.95
Season of Promises *Mitch Finley*	$4.95
Sometimes I Haven't Got a Prayer *Mary Sherry*	$8.95
St. Katharine Drexel *Daniel McSheffery*	$12.95
Stay with Us *John Mullin, SJ*	$3.95
What He Did for Love *Francis X. Gaeta*	$5.95
Woman Soul *Pat Duffy, OP*	$7.95
You Are My Beloved *Mitch Finley*	$10.95

For a free catalog call 1-800-892-6657
www.catholicbookpublishing.com